The 1Shanthiroad Cookbook

Edited by Suresh Jayaram

The 1Shanthiroad Cookbook
Edited by Suresh Jayaram

Reliable Copy #4
Second Edition – 2000

Consulting Editor: Anita Rao Kashi
Copy Editors: Thanik Jaganath and Stuti Bhavsar
Publication Design: Roshan Shakeel
Illustrations: Akshay Sethi
Cover Graphic: Suresh Jayaram
Researchers: Nihaal Faizal and Sarasija Subramanian
Research Assistants: Manasa Kashi, Kumaraaditya Rao,
Koyal Raheja, and Sneha Joshi

reliable copy

The 1Shanthiroad Cookbook has been made possible through the generous support of Rubamin Foundation, in association with Gallery Ark, Vadodara and Goethe-Institut / Max Mueller Bhavan, Bangalore.

Research towards this book was made possible with support from India Foundation for the Arts under the Arts Research Grant.

 India Foundation for the Arts

The production of the first edition of this book was supported by Universal Thirst and the ArtVarta Publishing Grant from Akar Prakar, in association with the Lath Sarvodaya Trust.

Copyright © Contributors, Suresh Jayaram, and Reliable Copy, 2020
Second edition, 2022

All rights reserved. No part of this publication may be reproduced, stored in retrieval systems, or transmitted by any form, by any means, without the prior permissions of the copyright owner.

Printed by: Sudarsan Graphics, Chennai

ISBN: 978-81-953472-6-1

Suresh Jayaram and Reliable Copy would like to thank Aaiushi Beniwal, Aishwaryan K, Amshu Chukki, Anita Rao Kashi, Ankit Ravani, Anna Mary Magdalene, Archana Hande, Arshad Hakim, Arshi Irshad Ahmadzai, Arundhati Ghosh, Arunesh Maiyar, Ashok Vish, Ayisha Abraham, Babu Eshwar Prasad, Barblina Meierhans, Basavachar S, Benjamin Buchanan, Bharathesh GD, Bhavani GS, Birte Hendricks, Biju Cherayath, Bilal Javeed, Devi Raju, Dimple B Shah, George Demir, Heena Pari, Dr. Hemalatha Bhuvanendra, Jahangir Asgar Jani, Janet Burchill & Jennifer McCamley, Janet Meaney, Jayasimha Chandrashekar, Julia D Kjelgaard, Kadamboor Neeraj, Dr. Lakshmi Devi, Lina Vincent, Manasa Kashi, Mandy Ridley, Mariraj Rajasekaran, Maureen Gonsalves, Miya Shivaram, Mohanavathi V, Murari Jha, Muskaan Singh, NS Harsha, Nihaal Faizal, Omana Eappen, Pradeep Kambathalli, Pushpamala N, Raghu Tenkayala, Ragini Bhow, Ramalingam VK, Renu Appachu, Ricardo Gallego, Rohini Sen, Rucha Vibhute, Sandeep TK, Sapna Chandu, Sarasija Subramanian, Shanthi Kasi, Sheela Gowda, Shiva Syam, Shivaji Panikkar, Shubham Kumar, Shyamli Singbal, Sitikanta Samantsinghar, Smitha Cariappa, Sohail Abdullah, Sunil Sigdel, Thisath Thoradeniya, Thomas & Renée Rapedius, Tim Wolfgarten, Tsohil Bhatia, Umesh Kumar, Uwe Jonas, and Yugashri Anandappa for their recipe contributions towards the book.

Suresh Jayaram and Reliable Copy would also like to thank Ala Younis & Kayfa-ta, Amit Kumar Jain, Anjolie Singh, Anna-Sophie Springer & K. Verlag, Arshad Hakim, Arshi Irshad Ahmadzai, Bilal Javeed, Christine Rogers, Heena Pari, Janet Burchill & Jennifer McCamley, Julia D Kjelgaard & F Stephen Dobson, Junpei Mori, Kalapi Gajjar-Bordawekar & Universal Thirst, Mandy Ridley, Nishi Chauhan, Shaunak Mahbubani, Shun Owada & Maaru Hiyama, Siri Khandavilli, Tim Wolfgarten & George Demir, Vasundhara Sellamuthu, Yukari Koyama, Yuko Nexus6, Yuu Yamamoto, and Zarine & Mohammed Faizal for having supported the production of the first edition of this book.

Contents

FOREWORD ... 13
INTRODUCTION TO THE COOKBOOK ... 17

BREAKFAST ... 21

23 Sweet Pongal
24 Khaara Pongal
25 Puttu
26 Nuchinunde
27 Oats Dosa
28 Kancheepuram Idli
30 Ragi Pancakes
31 Dressed-up Chapatis
32 Spanish Omelette
33 French Toast Bake
34 Fatafat Omelette

SNACKS ... 37

39 Congress Kadlekai Masala
40 Masala Boiled Eggs
41 Kadale Sundal
42 Pidi Kozhakattai
43 Seasoned Kozhakattai
44 Khaara Kadubu
46 Sweet Kadubu
48 Alasande Vada
49 Sabudana Vada
51 Fulaura
52 Arbi Cutlets
54 Khandvi
56 Potato Mustard Baked Chips

SOUPS AND SALADS ... 59

61 Zucchini and Pea Soup with Basil
62 Beetroot Soup
64 Kosambari
65 Welcome to Paradise
67 Half-Moon in the Forest Salad
69 Pikachu Salad

MAINS ... 73

75 Spanish Paella
78 Stir-fried Veggies with Pasta
79 Pasta with Sausage, Basil, and Mustard Sauce
80 Capellini with Tomato Pesto
82 Stuffed Capsicum Bake
83 Christmas Nut Roast
84 Azerbaijan Stuffed Spiral Bread
86 Ratatouille
87 Roast Beef with Mashed Potatoes and Sauerkraut
90 Beef Tongue with Olives
91 Mutton Thalki
92 Kashmiri Yakhni

93 Khichra
95 Chemmeen Roast
96 Kozhi Ularthiyathu
98 Undhiyo
102 Litti Chokha

CURRIES AND GRAVIES 107

109 Nadan Kozhi Thengapal Curry
111 Tamarind Chicken
113 Usha Bhandari's Chicken Saaru
115 Chicken Afghani
116 Kashmiri Chicken Curry
117 Kamala's Chicken Makhani
119 Varutharacha Meen Curry
120 Sri Lankan Fish Curry
122 Tomato Fish Curry
123 Mithila Fish Curry
125 Bangdache Hooman
127 Gwadri Machi Bhatt
129 Paragon Prawn Mango Curry
131 Pandi Curry
132 Sopan Muller's Avial
133 Vegetable Stew
135 Butter and Milk Vegetable
136 Ishwar's Vegetable Kadhi
140 Kenyan Channa Bateta
142 Lakshmi Devi's Vegetable Korma
143 Devi's Vegetable Korma
145 Mudre Kanni
147 Lakshmi Devi's Vada Curry
148 Manga Kutaan
150 Beetroot Rasam
151 Sumana's Gokarna Kai Rasa
155 Sumana's Gokarna Sambrani
159 Gauri Lankesh's Urgent Saaru
160 Soppu Cream Saaru
161 Raw Jackfruit Curry
162 Baimbale Curry
163 Pineapple Curry
164 Pappu
165 Bele Saaru
166 Bassaaru
168 3-in-1 Bassaaru, Palya, and Chutney
170 Avarekai Masale Saaru
172 Molake Hulli

RICE AND STAPLES 175

177 Bhakri
178 Akki Rotti
179 Masale Akki Rotti
181 Ragi Mudde
182 Kadambuttu
183 Akki Tari
184 Coconut Milk Pulao
185 Sunday Pulao
186 Menthya Palav
187 Masale Bath
188 Chicken Biryani
190 Asmi Bhabhi's Fish Biryani
192 Ummima's Jhinge jo Hao

ACCOMPANIMENTS 195

197 Vegetable Stir-fry
199 Potato Stir-fry
200 Beetroot Palya
201 Quick Thondekai Palya

202 Padavalanga Thoran
203 Achinga Mezhukkupuratti
204 Achinga Mezhukkupuratti with a Twist
206 Spinach Sabzi
207 Raw Banana Poriyal
208 Sweet Potato Poriyal
209 Ridge Gourd with Peanut Masala
210 Tamilian Brinjal Masala
211 Sumana's Bendekai Palya
214 Sumana's Bendekai Saasme
219 Pithala
221 Nellikai Tambli
223 Curd Curry

DIPS 227

229 Curd and Dill Dip
230 Beetroot Dip
231 Hummus
232 Avocado and Raw Mango Dip
233 Pomegranate Dip
234 Curry Leaf Dip

CHUTNEYS 237

239 Sweet and Sour Mango Chutney
240 Coconut Chutney
241 Coconut Fried Gram Chutney
242 Peanut Chutney
243 Coco-mint Chutney
244 Horse Gram Chutney
245 Heerekai Chutney
246 Raw Mango Chutney
247 Gongura Chutney
248 Thecha

PICKLES AND RELISHES 251

253 Nelikkai Thokku
254 Chintakaya Thokku
255 Prawn Dosakaya Pickle
256 Raw Mango Pickle
257 Raw Black Pepper Pickle
258 Jajju Mullangi
259 Puliyodharai Mix
260 Puli Inji
261 Sumana's Gokarna Heerekai Gojju
264 Tomato Gojju
265 Banana Rasayana
266 Chilli Peanut Butter

SWEETS AND DESSERTS 269

271 Kajjaaya
272 Hollige
273 Peanut Coconut Barfi
275 Bamboo Rice Payasam
276 Koovale Puttu
277 Fruit Custard
278 Tender Coconut Pudding
279 Chocolate Olive Oil Cake
281 Gluten-free Chocolate Cake with Almond Flour
283 Orange Cardamom Cake
285 Citrus Semolina Cake
286 Cooker Cake
288 Fudgy Brownies

290 Coffee Cake
291 Rich Christmas Fruit Cake
293 Black Forest Cookies
294 Peanut Butter Blossom Cookies

BEVERAGES 297

299 Rum Punch
300 Sangria
302 Painkiller
303 Cuba Libre
304 Blood and Sand
305 Jalapeño/Chilli-Infused Margarita
306 Pomegranate Lime Vodka Cocktail
307 Hot Toddy
308 Spiced Rum

PODIS AND FRESH MASALAS 311

313 South Karnataka Chutney Pudi
315 Flax Seed Chutney Pudi
317 Dry Peanut Chutney
318 Kovakkai Poriyal Masala
319 Bachelor Sambhar Powder
320 Pepper Rasam Powder
321 Upaddam Podi
322 Kara Kozhambu Masala

GLOSSARY 325
CONTRIBUTORS 333

Foreword

My grandmother, Krishnamma, and her niece, Puttakka, lived in a traditional South Indian home with a large courtyard and kitchen garden which was constantly buzzing with activity. She was an elegant and saintly woman who was born in Mavalli, adjacent to the Lalbagh Botanical Garden. My grandfather, Varadhappa, was an agriculturist who owned vineyards and vegetable gardens in Hoskote (on the outskirts of Bangalore) where he grew 'English' vegetables. My summer holidays were spent with them and I have many vivid memories of my grandmother's kitchen. One of the earliest is of sitting cross-legged on the floor and eating from a small raised stool called *peeta*. I always looked forward to my visits to this house with excitement—to experience the open kitchen and rummage through her storeroom for seeds and knick-knacks, amidst brass vessels, lanterns, large pickle jars, and terracotta granaries. Every season I witnessed the collective harvest, swam in the water tank, and picked blue grapes that were sent to the city markets (to be made into sweet wine and jams for sandwiches).

The food tasted different in her home—simple and nutritious. The ingredients were foraged from the open *maidan*, like the freshly plucked spinach, boiled and garnished with chilli, garlic, and grated coconut to make the *busdida saaru* or *soppina saaru* that we would eat with hot *ragi mudde*. I was meticulously taught to eat the *mudde* under my grandmother's supervision—instructed to dip the hot *ragi* ball in the curry and swallow without chewing. My relatives devoured this native delicacy with ease, but they were sympathetic and taught me the etiquette of eating without messing one's hands and without wasting a morsel of food.

There were no machines and the only sign of modernity was an electric bulb. A variety of grinding stones (*chakkis*) were used to make medicines, spicy chutneys, and *masalas* for curries. The food was cooked on wood-fire, in terracotta pots glazed with use. The silver and brass vessels glistened in the light of the flame, etching the distinctively smoky flavour they lent to dishes forever in my memory.

My grandmother came from a traditional household, where the entire process of cooking, serving, and eating was transformed into *sadhana*—a spiritual practice. Eating was considered a sacred act that nourished the body and soul, enlivening the web of life. After the harvest festival in the village, a share of the produce was given away. It was not seen as charity, but instead as a way of life—*dharma*; to see others as oneself and the world as family—*vasudeva kutumbakam*. The food was served on banana leaves and a *shloka* was recited before starting the meal. This ritual made the food sacred and guests blessed the host by saying *Annadata Sukhi Bhava*, which translates to "may those who provide me with this food remain happy."

Krishnamma lived a hundred years and left behind many treasures for her grandchildren. To me, came a granite *chakki* that reminds me of her and the songs she used to sing while grinding grains in the kitchen. Her life of abundance was a lesson for us in spirituality, sustainability, and sharing. My mother wanted us to learn from her way of life which was simple and connected; a reality rooted in the living traditions of an agrarian household. These interactions and conversations have always stayed with me and were also a constant inspiration for my mother who inherited and embodied this tradition of keeping an open house.

My mother, Lakshmi Devi, was the first doctor in the family. She was married to Jayaram, a political advisor and socialist who relished food. I grew up seeing my father hovering in the kitchen, chopping onions, peeling garlic, or shelling peas. He was more of a *rasika* of food than a cook himself; his task was the shopping—he knew where to get the freshest vegetables and choicest of fruits from the *mandi*, and the best meat from his favorite butchers.

The kitchen in our house led to a backyard garden with fresh herbs, a few seasonal vegetables, and most importantly, a curry leaf tree—adapting the joys of my grandmother's agrarian household to an urban setting. My mother would mainly cook on the weekends, employed as she was the rest of the week. While she was very particular about following exact cooking procedures and methods, she was also very good at improvising recipes using leftovers from the day before, mixing and matching things to make something that often tasted even better.

In fact, her food acquired a legendary reputation, and family and friends would travel great distances to come and eat her famous coconut-based curries, *biryanis*, coconut rice with mutton chops, vegetarian curries, prawns, and fish. She always remembered what each person enjoyed the most and made it a point to cook their favourites when they visited. In the summers, aunts and cousins would pour in, helping my mother grind fresh *masalas* for *sambhars*, *rasams*, and curries, pickling vegetables and spices, and drying condiments and *papads* in the sun.

I was assigned the role of the taster and I learnt how to savour flavours and understand complex dishes by tasting them and trying to figure out what was missing. I did not write down any of the recipes, but instead memorised them by observing my mother, grandmother, uncles, and aunts in the kitchen. Recreating them in my own kitchen became an art I perfected by recalling these memories and cooking each dish again and again till they matched my recollection of tastes and smells. Although I could never match their skills in the kitchen, I inherited from them the love of cooking and serving.

When I built 1Shanthiroad, I imagined it as a revolving salon for artists; a public-private space—an extension of the open house tradition that I grew up in. Very often, I hear visitors wondering if there are any demarcations within the spaces at 1Shanthiroad, but these have been consciously blurred to produce multiple possibilities. For instance, the drawing room opens out to two courtyards which act as spillover spaces from the public gallery. One is shaded by a benevolent *badam* tree and the other has a mezzanine floor hovering over the space. These courtyards draw the winds and have become spaces for people to congregate, collaborate, and create.

The kitchen in my house is small and compact, designed according to my needs by my architect Meeta Jain. It was never meant for cooking lavish feasts for large groups of people, but its open plan makes it a part of the modestly-sized living space, allowing for a sense of informality that is part of the ethos of 1Shanthiroad. An old Kanjeevaram saree hangs as a screen, a kind of homage to my mother, witnessing these endless collaborations. Those interested pop into the kitchen to help cook, and the openness allows artists and visitors to become a part of the ritual of stirring the quintessential rum punch, making dips or chutneys, or chopping for salads.

Since its inception, the food at 1Shanthiroad has been made by Devi Raju, the cook initially employed by a friend who rented a space downstairs. She has been supported by Mohanavathi V (Mona), the caretaker and an integral member of the 1Shanthiroad family. Whenever there is a show opening, performance, or lecture in the evening, I also cook something quick, mostly a snack. I have realised that I don't want to grind *masalas* or get into tedious ways of cooking, but rather prefer to cook quick food that is tasty, nourishing, and can be prepared in large batches. I tend to make things that are easy and light on the stomach, like stir-fries, soups, salads, and dips—and these staples of mine are the ones that have become my contribution to the cookbook.

Of course, the occasional curries learnt from my mother seep into my kitchen, and I have also borrowed from her a way of cooking quick meals from leftovers. As a result, the menu at 1Shanthiroad is eclectic, and these days largely vegetarian, as per my preference.

There is one large dining table in 1Shanthiroad where people gather to eat, which morphs into a work table just after the meal. A private dining experience here is rare, as it only occurs when I am alone. As a result, my home has been called a soup kitchen, railway station waiting room, an art-ashram for crazy creative beings, and a home for lost souls and hungry stomachs. It is difficult for me to cook for just one or two people because here I have gotten used to cooking for more than ten people at a time. The belief that more is good has stayed with me, since guests pop in unexpectedly quite often.

Food is a lubricant that makes things move and sustains 1Shanthiroad as a growing community of people. It brings us together and sparks conversations among different cultures. I feel that without the shared meals, 1Shanthiroad would not be what it is today—an extension of my mother's house of plenty and an ever expanding *akshayapatra* that brims with the spirit of sharing and generosity.

Never for a second was it imagined that such a small kitchen could feed so many that come and go, each bringing their own stories to share. Making space for art would have never been possible without this kitchen, which became the studio where we use all our senses. Cooking is unmistakably an art that involves the whole body and in turn we become a part of it. My mother, who lived downstairs, once came up to the studio and gave me the greatest compliment I have received. She said, "you are continuing the family tradition of cooking and feeding everyone." There's no life without food and this pot of plenty keeps overflowing with the grace of my family who encouraged me to live this bohemian life and to keep my doors open for the world to pass through. Many have asked me what the secret to the food is. The answer is simple—the secret is sharing.

Introduction to the Cookbook

The idea for this cookbook began as a tiny spark over a year ago during a dinner with friends at 1Shanthiroad. It took on a life of its own and became a mammoth project involving 77 contributors from across 4 continents. It reflects the diversity of people who have passed through the doors of 1Shanthiroad in terms of culture, geography, and sensibilities. Inevitably, this has meant a smorgasbord of flavours, textures, ingredients, and methods.

Predictably, with so many people involved, the making of this book has been marked by several serendipitous occasions. Old friendships were rekindled and dishes long forgotten were resurrected. In keeping with this unconventional process, it was only right that Akshay Sethi, an artist who was in residence during the early stages of the book's production, became an integral part of the process. His illustrations populate the book, representing the space through the assortment of objects that trigger memories of the many nooks and corners of 1Shanthiroad.

Food is highly individual, often a matter of pride and also a product of its roots. We have tried to protect those attributes as far as possible, while bringing in enough uniformity to make this book usable and engaging, with the help of Anita Rao Kashi, a food and travel writer and regular visitor to 1Shanthiroad who joined the project in its last stages.

For all the bits of their milieu that different kinds of people have each brought to the kitchen of 1Shanthiroad, it is undoubtedly entrenched in the local community and culture of Karnataka. It is astonishing how variegated the dishes have been, even in such a small subset, and perhaps a bit confusing at first. You will encounter *sambhar, saaru, bassaaru, hulli,* and *rasam*—all variations of one another, but also different in usage based on geographic region, community, and a myriad of other factors. Hopefully, while exciting and satiating your taste buds, each of these will also aim a bit higher—to kindle curiosity and inform about some aspect of the dish's ethnic grounding.

As mentioned earlier, we did attempt to bring some uniformity to the recipes but in ways that do not affect the cultural ethos of a dish. A casual glance might suggest that we have done a temperamental job of translating terms but there's a reason for it—some words, like *puttu,* or *fulaura,* or *kajjaaya,* or *undhiyo,* are simply untranslatable. Explanations would have been clunky and reductive; instead, we chose to protect the inherent idiosyncrasies of the dishes. Perhaps that will encourage you to look them up, and hopefully try them.

That said, of course, we are not going to leave you floundering. At the end of the book is a fairly extensive glossary of most ingredients, as well as some equipment, with equivalents in three languages—English, Hindi, and Kannada. Beyond that, there's always the digital route.

These pages are also peppered with the quirks, philosophies, biographical digressions, and even diktat-like directions of the authors. Hopefully, this book becomes dog-eared, smudged with oil, smeared with turmeric and chocolate, and eventually infused with the aromas of the dishes it contains within its pages. After all, that's the true purpose of a family cookbook.

BREAKFAST

Sweet Pongal ✦ Khaara Pongal ✦ Puttu ✦ Nuchinunde ✦ Oats Dosa ✦ Kancheepuram Idli ✦ Ragi Pancakes ✦ Dressed-up Chapatis ✦ Spanish Omelette ✦ French Toast Bake ✦ Fatafat Omelette

Sweet Pongal

Dr. Hemalatha Bhuvanendra

Serves 2

125 g rice
125 g *moong dal*
600 ml water
250 g jaggery powder
1 glass milk
½ coconut

TEMPERING:
25 g raisins
25 g cashew nuts
2 tbsp *ghee*

Dry roast rice and *moong dal* separately. In case of *moong dal*, roast until it is golden-brown. Grate coconut and keep aside.

Cook the roasted rice and *moong dal* in a pressure cooker for two whistles in double the amount of water (approximately 600 ml). Once the pressure is released, open and let it cool. Once it cools (in about 10 minutes), add jaggery, milk, and grated coconut and boil for 10 to 15 minutes.

Heat 2 tbsp of *ghee* in a *kadhai*. Fry raisins and cashew nuts until the cashew nuts turn golden-brown. Add this to the *pongal* and stir well.

Serve hot with *ghee*.

Notes:
—This sweet is made during Sankranti festival, usually accompanied by *khaara pongal*.

Khaara Pongal

(Savoury Pongal)

Dr. Hemalatha Bhuvanendra

Serves 2

125 g rice
125 g *moong dal*
600 ml water
4 green chillies
1 thumb-sized piece of ginger
2 onions
1 tsp mustard seeds
½ tsp cumin seeds
1 sprig of curry leaves
2 tsp oil
1 tsp salt

GARNISH:
1 tbsp *ghee*
25 g cashew nuts
A handful of coriander leaves

Dry roast rice and *moong dal* separately. In case of *moong dal*, roast until it is golden-brown. Finely chop ginger, green chillies, and onions and keep aside.

Cook the roasted rice and *moong dal* in a pressure cooker for two whistles in double the amount of water (approximately 600 ml). Once the pressure is released, open and let it cool.

In a pan, add 2 tsp of oil and fry mustard seeds and cumin seeds. When they start to splutter, add curry leaves, green chillies, and ginger. Then add onions and fry until they become soft and pink. Then add the cooked rice-*dal* mix, a glass of water, and 1 tsp of salt and cook for 15 to 20 minutes.

In a separate *kadhai*, heat *ghee* and fry cashew nuts until they turn golden-brown. Garnish the *pongal* with fried cashews and finely-chopped coriander leaves.

Serve hot with *ghee*.

Puttu

Sandeep TK

Serves 4

1 cup coarse rice flour
1 coconut
3½ cups water
Salt to taste

Grate coconut and keep aside. Take rice flour in a bowl and add ¼ tsp of salt. Sprinkle some water and mix it well. To the bottom of the *puttu kudam*, add about 3 cups of water and heat on a stove over medium flame. Wait until the water boils.

Place the perforated disc at the base of the cylinder and then start filling it. First put in about 3 tbsp of grated coconut and then fill in rice powder till the cylinder is half-full. Add another 3 tbsp of grated coconut, fill in the rest of the cylinder with rice powder, and top with the last 3 tbsp of grated coconut. Then close the cylinder and place on top of the *kudam*. Cook for 9 to 10 minutes until you smell the fragrant mix of coconut and rice flour. Switch off the gas and carefully remove the cylinder. Be cautious since it will be very hot—wear gloves if required. Use a wooden spoon to push out the *puttu*.

Traditionally served with *kadala* curry or steamed bananas.

Notes:
—*Puttu kudam*: A vessel with a bottom portion in the shape of a *kudam (*pot), that acts as the base, and a top portion that is cylindrical. The top is used to fill in the rice flour. This is an essential requirement for this recipe.

—In the first step of the process, the texture of the rice flour mix is really important—when you make a small lump of this mixture and break it, it must crumble. This is the form you need to achieve.

—The *puttu kudam* does not make a sound (like a pressure cooker), so you have to be attentive to the fragrance.

Nuchinunde

Bhavani GS

Serves 5–6

½ cup *chana dal*
½ cup *toor dal*
¼ cup *urad dal*
1 onion
1–2 green chillies
½-inch piece of ginger
5–6 curry leaves
1 cup finely-chopped dill leaves
½ cup finely-chopped coriander leaves
¼ cup grated coconut
2–3 tsp oil
Salt to taste

Soak all the *dals* for 2 hours. Grind the soaked *toor dal* and *chana dal* coarsely and the *urad dal* finely, without adding water. Finely chop onion, green chillies, ginger, and curry leaves.

Mix the above ingredients with dill leaves, coriander leaves, grated coconut, and salt to taste, together in a bowl. Make small oval-shaped dumplings of this mixture in your fist. Keep aside.

Take a pressure cooker (or a large pot) and add a cup of water. Grease perforated plates (or *idli* plates) with a few drops of oil and place 6 to 8 of these dumplings on each. Place these plates in the pot, cover and steam for 15 to 20 minutes.

Serve hot with coconut chutney and *ghee*.

Oats Dosa

Shanthi Kasi

Serves 1

4 tbsp rolled oats
1 tbsp semolina
1 tbsp wheat flour
1 onion
1 green chilli
½ carrot
1 sprig of curry leaves
A handful of coriander leaves
Salt to taste
Oil for making *dosas*

Finely chop onion, coriander leaves, curry leaves, and green chilli. Grate carrot. In a bowl, mix the chopped vegetables and greens with the rolled oats, semolina, wheat flour, and salt. Add water to this, little by little, continuously mixing it till the batter becomes consistent. Keep the batter aside for about 30 minutes to soak.

Grease an iron *tawa* or non-stick pan with oil and heat on the stove. Once hot, add a ladle-full of the *dosa* batter and spread evenly. Drizzle a little oil on top and let the *dosa* cook until brown on both sides.

Serve with green chutney or curd.

Notes:
—The first *dosa* is invariably a trial to test the heat of the non-stick pan or the *tawa*—it may stick or break.

—The *dosas* are to be made as one would make regular *dosas*, only the texture of this batter is a bit rough.

—The oats tend to absorb water as it soaks. If required, add a little extra water before making the *dosas*.

—This recipe was taught to me by Sujata Iyer, a friend whom I stayed with during my residency at 1Shanthiroad.

Kancheepuram Idli

Shanthi Kasi

Makes 12 idlis

1 cup raw rice (*idli* rice)
1 cup *urad dal*
Salt to taste

SEASONING:
2–3 tsp oil
1 tsp mustard seeds
2 tsp black peppercorns
10–12 curry leaves
2 tbsp grated ginger
2 tsp roughly-chopped cashew nuts

Mix rice and *urad dal* and rinse 2 to 3 times with water. Let the mixture soak overnight. The next morning, grind it in a mixer-grinder. This ground batter should be slightly rough in texture. Add salt and let it ferment for 8 to 10 hours.

In a pan, heat a few spoons of oil and add mustard seeds. Once they splutter, add in peppercorns, curry leaves, grated ginger, and cashew nuts and fry. Pour this into the fermented batter and mix well.

Grease *idli* plates with a few drops of oil and pour in the batter. Steam for 10 to 15 minutes. Alternatively, put the batter in a deep pan dish and steam for approximately 7 minutes. Once cool, cut into pieces for serving.

Serve with *podi, sambhar,* and chutney.

Notes:
—Kancheepuram is a famous temple town located in South India. It is famous for its temple architecture, silk *saris*, and its *idlis*! This *idli* variant is made at the Sri Varadaraja Perumal temple as an offering to the deities. The origin is unknown, but is believed to have been offered to the deities from the times of the Pallava Dynasty.

—Traditionally steamed in dried *mantharai* leaves (Bauhinia variegata/

kachnar/ manthara) and over a wood fire, Kancheepuram *idlis* are cylindrical in shape. Those made at the temple are around a foot long and cut into discs for serving.

—The recipe has been adapted for home preparation. Some may add cumin seeds and coriander leaves instead of mustard seeds and curry leaves; the basic spirit of the *idli* is nevertheless retained.

Ragi Pancakes

(Finger Millet Pancakes)

Suresh Jayaram

Serves 6

BATTER:
1 cup *urad dal*
2 cups *ragi* flour
A pinch of salt

TOPPINGS:
1 cup grated coconut
½ cup roasted peanuts
Jaggery powder to taste
1 tsp cinnamon powder
4 ripe bananas

6 tsp *ghee* or butter

Soak *urad dal* overnight. Rinse well and grind to a fine paste. Mix *ragi* flour with water until it achieves the consistency of pancake batter, making sure there are no lumps. To this mix, add the ground *urad dal* and a pinch of salt. Set the batter aside for 3 to 4 hours to ferment.

For the topping, mix jaggery powder, grated coconut, crushed roasted peanuts, and cinnamon powder and keep aside. Chop bananas into discs.

Heat a *tawa*, make a large pancake with the batter, and drizzle a spoon of *ghee* or butter over and around it. Cover the pan and let it cook for a few minutes on a reduced flame. Once the pancake is cooked, top it with a few pieces of banana, 1 tbsp of the topping mixture and fold the pancake in half.

Serve hot with honey.

Notes:
—If the batter does not seem to have fermented, add a pinch of baking soda.

Dressed-up Chapatis

Dr. Lakshmi Devi

Serves 2

1 cup wheat flour
1 egg
1½ cups milk
¼ tsp salt
5 tbsp oil

Sift flour and salt into a bowl. Make a well in the centre, break in an egg, and pour in a third of the milk. Stir and beat well, until smooth. Gradually blend in the remaining milk. Keep aside for at least 20 minutes and stir again before using.

Heat a frying pan and smear with a cloth dipped in oil. Pour in sufficient batter to cover the base of the pan, and tilt so that the batter spreads evenly. Cook gently without moving the pan, until the underside of the crêpe is golden-brown. Turn using a flat spatula, and cook the other side for about 5 minutes.

Serve hot with honey.

Spanish Omelette

Devi Raju

Serves 8–10

7 potatoes
1 onion
10 eggs
½ tsp black pepper powder
Salt to taste
1 ½ ladles of oil

Thinly slice potatoes and finely chop the onion. In a large bowl, crack and beat eggs until they become light and fluffy. Keep aside.

Heat 2 tbsp of oil in a pan and add chopped onion. Cook until translucent and add sliced potatoes. Cook until they are soft, remove from flame, mash into smaller pieces with a wooden spoon, and cool. Add this mash into the beaten eggs, along with salt and pepper.

Heat 2 tsp of oil in a non-stick pan, making sure it is evenly coated. Once hot, pour in a ladleful of the egg mixture and spread evenly, but thickly (to approximately 1-inch thickness). Cook for a few minutes until the omelette is firm and golden-brown. Flip it over onto a plate, and slide back to cook the other side. Use a fork to poke holes in the omelette to make sure it cooks from within. Repeat with the remaining egg mixture to make more servings.

Serve hot.

Notes:
—This recipe was learnt from Ricardo Gallego's mother who was visiting from Spain while I was employed as a cook at his residence,

French Toast Bake

Ashok Vish

Serves 6–8

½ cup butter
1 cup brown sugar
1 loaf of thick bread
4 eggs
½ cup milk
1 tsp vanilla essence
½ cup powdered sugar

Melt butter in a microwave and add brown sugar to it. Stir until the sugar completely dissolves. Pour this mixture onto the bottom of a 9 x 13-inch baking dish and spread evenly.

In a bowl, beat together eggs, milk, and vanilla essence. Cut slices of bread in half. Lay a single layer of the cut bread in the baking dish on the butter mixture. Now, spoon ½ the prepared egg mixture over the layer of bread. Top this with a second layer of cut bread, followed by a topping of the remaining egg mixture. Cover the baking dish with foil and refrigerate overnight. The next morning, bake at 175 degrees Celsius for 45 minutes—covered for the first 30 minutes and open for the subsequent 15.

Serve with sprinkled powdered sugar and warm maple syrup.

Fatafat Omelette

Pradeep Kambathalli

Serves 2

4 eggs
A dash of red chilli powder
Salt to taste
2–3 tbsp groundnut oil
A pinch of oregano seasoning

As this is a very quick dish and doesn't take much preparation, gather all the ingredients and keep them close by. Take a *tawa* and heat it on a stove on high flame for approximately a minute, and then reduce the flame to medium and spread ½ tbsp of oil on the *tawa* with an oil brush/spoon.

Break open the eggs in the area where you have spread the oil. You will hear the familiar and pleasing sizzle as it spreads. Do not mix the eggs, let it spread the way it wants to. Just make sure it is approximately round in shape as it will be easier to flip it over. After about 25 seconds, add a dash of chilli powder on top along with a sprinkling of salt to taste. Give it 5 more seconds, and then flip it. Let it stay on the *tawa* for another 10 seconds, and *voilà*, it's done!

Usually this dish is eaten straight out of the *tawa*, so I have never witnessed it being served. However, you can serve it on a plate with a sprinkling of oregano seasoning, if available.

Notes:
—The oregano can be from the sachet which usually comes delivered with pizza.

—The preferred oil is groundnut, but coconut or refined vegetable oil can be used as well.

—It is also a great quick fix starter when having a beer or a late-night fix when roaming about in the house aimlessly.

—I learnt this recipe from Cop Shiva, during one of the Khoj Residency projects at 1Shanthiroad.

SNACKS

Congress Kadlekai Masala ✦ Masala Boiled Eggs ✦ Kadale Sundal ✦ Pidi Kozhakattai ✦ Seasoned Kozhakattai ✦ Khaara Kadubu ✦ Sweet Kadubu ✦ Alasande Vada ✦ Sabudana Vada ✦ Fulaura ✦ Arbi Cutlets ✦ Khandvi ✦ Potato Mustard Baked Chips

Congress Kadlekai Masala

(Congress Peanut Masala)

Suresh Jayaram

Serves 3–4

A handful of coriander leaves
2 large onions
2 limes
200 g split, roasted, and salted peanuts from the local bakery
1 tsp red chilli powder

Finely chop coriander leaves and onions. Mix them in a bowl with peanuts. Add chilli powder and squeeze in the juice of 2 limes. Mix all the ingredients.

Serve as a snack.

Notes:
—This dish gets its name from the historic split in the Congress Party in 1969 at Lalbagh, Bangalore, which inspired a local condiment shop to name this peanut snack 'Congress *kadlekai*'.

Masala Boiled Eggs

Suresh Jayaram

Serves 6

6 eggs
3 tbsp mustard seed paste
2 onions
1 small bunch of spring onions
1 tbsp black pepper powder
Salt to taste

Finely chop onions and spring onions. Hard-boil the eggs and peel them. Cut eggs into halves and remove the yolks. In a bowl, mash egg yolks and add in onions, mustard seed paste, pepper, and salt, and mix well. Fill the mixture back into the halved eggs.

Serve garnished with chopped spring onions.

Notes:
—Spring onions can be replaced with dill leaves for a different flavour.

Kadale Sundal

(Chickpea Sundal)

Ramalingam VK

Serves 6–8

250 g chickpeas
½ coconut
1 raw mango
1 carrot
4 green chillies
1 sprig of curry leaves
2 tbsp coriander leaves
1 tsp mustard seeds
2 pinches of asafoetida
2 dry red chillies
3 tbsp refined oil
Salt to taste

Soak chickpeas overnight. The next day, cook them in a pressure cooker for three to four whistles until they are tender. Grate coconut, raw mango, and carrots. Finely chop green chillies and coriander leaves.

Heat oil in a pan and add mustard seeds. Once the mustard seeds splutter, add red chillies (broken in half), asafoetida, curry leaves, and green chillies, in this order. To this, add the boiled chickpeas and toss. Add grated carrots and raw mango, along with salt to taste. Toss well for 3 to 5 minutes on a low flame.

Serve garnished with grated coconut.

Notes:
—Chickpeas can be replaced with any whole lentils of your choice.

Pidi Kozhakattai

Ramalingam VK

Serves 6–8

3 cups broken rice
7 cups hot water
½ cup grated coconut
Salt to taste

MASALA:
6 dry red chillies
8 shallots
2 tsp oil
2 tsp mustard seeds
2 tbsp *urad dal*
6 green chillies
2 sprigs of curry leaves
1-inch piece of ginger

Grind shallots and red chillies in a mixer-grinder to a fine paste and keep aside. Finely chop green chillies and ginger.

Heat 2 tsp of oil in a saucepan and add mustard seeds, *urad dal*, green chillies, ginger, and curry leaves. Once tempered, add the paste made with shallots and red chilli. Add broken rice and sauté for 5 to 7 minutes. Add hot water and cook while constantly stirring, without allowing any lumps to form. Add grated coconut and salt to taste and cook till the rice is well done and has an *upma*-like consistency. Transfer to a large plate and cool.

After cooling, take small amounts of this mixture (enough to fit the palm of your hand) and press them tightly. Your palm and fingers acts as a mould to shape the dough. Keep these aside. Heat a steamer with hot water. Place the balls on a greased plate (or an *idli* plate) and steam for 10 to 15 minutes.

Serve hot as a snack.

Seasoned Kozhakattai

Aishwaryan K

Serves 4–6

500 g rice flour
1 small bowl hot water
1 coconut
Salt to taste

TEMPERING:
5–6 curry leaves
2–3 dry red chillies
1 tsp mustard seeds
2–3 green chillies
1 tsp *chana dal*
1 tsp *urad dal*
2 tsp vegetable or coconut oil

Grate coconut and keep aside. Mix rice flour and salt with hot water to make a soft dough. Divide into golf-ball-sized balls. Pinch each ball into the shape of a small cup and fill in with 1 tsp of grated coconut. After filling, seal each cup back into a ball.

Steam these balls in either a steamer or *idli* maker for 15 to 20 minutes. Once ready, cut them into halves or quarters, as preferred. Heat a pan with vegetable or coconut oil and add mustard seeds, *chana dal*, *urad dal*, broken red chillies, slit green chillies, and curry leaves. Slowly drop the steamed pieces and stir-fry till slightly crisp on the outside.

Sprinkle the remaining grated coconut and serve on its own or with chutney.

Khaara Kadubu

(Savoury Kadubu)

Dr. Hemalatha Bhuvanendra

Makes 15 pieces

300 g rice flour
1 cup water
2–3 tsp oil

FILLING:
50 g *chana dal*
4 green chillies
A handful of coriander leaves
2 cloves of garlic
1 thumb-sized piece of ginger
4 cloves
2 small cinnamon sticks
2 medium-sized onions
3 tbsp *ghee*
Salt to taste

Soak *chana dal* overnight. Chop green chillies, garlic, ginger, and coriander leaves, and finely chop onions.

Drain the *chana dal* and retain the water separately. Grind *dal* with green chillies, coriander leaves, garlic, ginger, cloves, and cinnamon in a mixer-grinder to form a thick coarse paste. To this paste, add the finely-chopped onions and salt.

Heat a thick-bottomed pan and add ½ a cup of the water that the *chana dal* was soaked in, a few drops of oil, and 1 tbsp of rice flour. Keep adding rice flour to the water in small quantities and use a foot long wooden stick (or ladle) to stir constantly until it thickens. For this step, use about 250 g of the rice flour. The final consistency should be that of porridge. Close the lid for 5 to 7 minutes and let it cook. Then take the pan off the stove and let it cool.

Knead the thickened mixture to make sure there is no leftover rice flour. Remove the contents and transfer onto a wet plate. The water on the plate will make sure the dough does not stick.

Dip your hands in cold water and divide the mixture into golf-ball-sized balls. Take each ball, dip it into the remaining dry rice flour and pinch into the shape of a cup using your index finger and thumb. Add the ground paste into this cup and pinch the edges together gently so that the contents don't spill out.

Take a pressure cooker (or a large pot) with a cup of water. Grease a perforated plate (or an *idli* plate) with *ghee* and place 6 to 8 *kadubus* on it. Place this plate in the cooker, and cover and steam for 10 to 15 minutes.

Serve hot with chutney.

Sweet Kadubu

Dr. Hemalatha Bhuvanendra

Makes 25 pieces

750 g rice flour
1 cup water
2–3 tsp oil

FILLING:
125 g peanuts
125 g fried gram *dal*
125 g sesame seeds
125 g desiccated coconut
1 kg jaggery
3 tbsp *ghee*

Roast peanuts, fried gram *dal*, and sesame seeds separately (as they roast at different speeds) until they turn golden-brown. Grind all three together into a fine powder. Mix with finely-powdered jaggery and grated desiccated coconut.

Heat a thick-bottomed pan and add a cup of water, a few drops of oil, and 1 tbsp of rice flour. Keep adding rice flour to the water in small quantities and use a foot-long wooden stick (or ladle) to stir constantly until it thickens. For this step, use about 500 g of the rice flour. The final consistency should be that of porridge. Close the lid for 5 to 7 minutes and let it cook. Then take the pan off the stove and let it cool.

Knead the mixture to make sure there is no leftover rice flour. Remove the contents and transfer onto a wet plate. The water on the plate will make sure the dough does not stick.

Dip your hands in cold water and divide the mixture into golf-ball-sized balls. Take each ball, dip it into the remaining dry rice flour and pinch into the shape of a cup using your index finger and thumb. Add 1 tsp of the filling into this cup, and pinch together the edges gently so the contents don't spill out.

Take a pressure cooker (or a large pot) with a cup of water. Grease a perforated plate (or an *idli* plate) with *ghee* and place 6 to 8 *kadubus* on it. Place this plate in the pot, cover and steam for 10 to 15 minutes.

Serve hot, as a snack or sweet dish.

Notes:

—This dish is made in Karnataka during Ganesha festival.

—You can play with the design and shape of this sweet, using different sizes and shapes of the rice cup.

Alasande Vada

(Cowpeas Vada)

Raghu Tenkayala

Makes 25–30 pieces

1 kg *lobia*
2 onions
10–12 green chillies
1 tsp ginger-garlic paste
A handful of coriander leaves
Salt to taste
Oil for frying

Soak *lobia* for about 7 to 8 hours. Remove the remaining skin, if any, and wash thoroughly. Drain the water. Finely chop onions, coriander leaves, and green chillies.

Coarsely grind the washed *lobia*, onions, green chillies, and ginger-garlic paste in a wet grinder or mixer-grinder to make a batter. To this, add coriander leaves and salt to taste. Take a small portion of this batter, the size of a golf ball, and flatten it slightly on your palm. Use your thumb to make a hole in the centre and deep-fry in oil.

Serve hot with chutney.

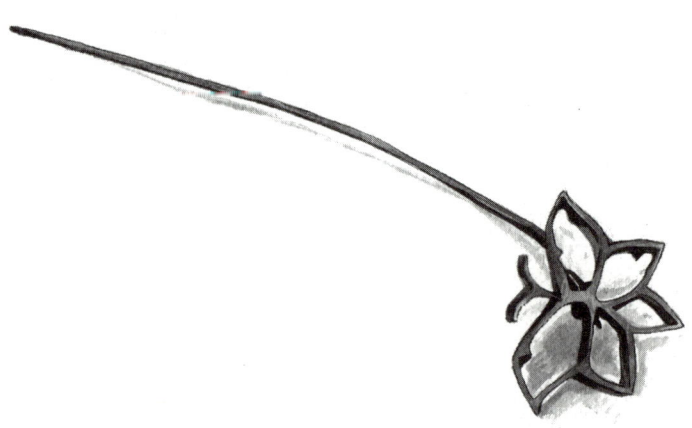

Sabudana Vada

(Tapioca Pearls Vada)

Shanthi Kasi

Makes 8–10 vadas

1 cup *sabudana*
¾ cup peanuts
2 large potatoes
Green chillies as per taste
1 tbsp cumin seeds
A few curry leaves
A few coriander leaves
Salt to taste
A pinch of sugar
200 ml oil

Take *sabudana* in a broad-based bowl and rinse it well with water, like you would rinse rice before cooking. After rinsing, add enough water to just cover the *sabudana*. Add a little sugar and salt, and let it soak for 6 to 8 hours (or overnight).

Dry roast peanuts, de-husk, and grind in a mixer-grinder to a coarse powder. Boil potatoes in a pressure cooker till they are well done. Drain the water, peel, and mash. Finely chop green chillies, coriander leaves, and curry leaves.

Mix all of the above ingredients, including cumin seeds, drained *sabudana*, and salt to taste, and make a stiff dough for the *vada*. Divide the dough into lime-sized balls, and flatten each in your palm to form patties approximately 2 inches in diameter.

Heat oil for frying in a heavy bottomed vessel or *kadhai*. To test the heat, put a pinch of the dough in the oil. If it rises quickly to the surface, it means that the oil is sufficiently heated. Deep-fry the patties on medium heat till golden-brown, and place on a paper towel to soak the excess oil.

Serve the *vadas* with green chutney or curd. It is best eaten when freshly fried and hot.

Notes:
—The *vadas* should be fried till they are crispy on the outside and soft on the inside. The mélange of textures is its key distinguishing feature.

— A vegan and gluten-free dish.

— This delicious creation originates in Maharashtra. It is one of the foods that is permitted whilst fasting and is known as *upvas vada*. It is filling as well as nutritious.

Fulaura

Sunil Sigdel

Serves 4

3 cups whole *urad* with husk
½ tbsp timur powder (Sichuan pepper powder)
½ tbsp red chilli powder
2 tsp turmeric powder
1½ tbsp ginger paste
Salt to taste
1 tbsp coriander-cumin powder
Oil for deep-frying

Soak *urad* overnight in cold water. The next day, drain water and clean the *urad* thoroughly. Blend *urad* in a mixer-grinder to a coarse paste. The consistency should be of thick pancake batter. Mix in timur powder, red chilli powder, turmeric powder, ginger paste, salt, and coriander-cumin powder.

Heat oil in a *kadhai* on medium heat and drop small lime-sized balls of the batter into the hot oil with your hand or spoon. Deep-fry these till they are golden-brown and crisp.

Serve hot with chutney, ketchup, or Sriracha sauce.

Notes:
—Timur powder can be replaced with black pepper powder.

—The first day of the month of Shravan is observed as the festival of Shravan Sankranti. It is a merry-making exercise after the busy period of paddy plantation. Families invite their married daughters and sisters, and celebrate together by laying out a variety of festival food. One of the dishes served is *fulaura*. In the evening, people celebrate Luto Phalne by burning wood and a plant called *tite pati*, and throwing it away shouting "*Luto laija*" ("take away scabies") to ward off the disease and the itching it causes.

Arbi Cutlets

(Taro Root Cutlets)

Sarasija Subramanian &
Kadamboor Neeraj

Serves 6–8

1 kg *arbi*
10–12 tbsp cooking oil
1 cup semolina

MASALA:
2 tbsp sesame seeds
2 tbsp *chana dal*
2 tbsp *urad dal*
4 dry red chillies
A pinch of asafoetida

TEMPERING:
6 tbsp sesame oil
1 tbsp coriander seeds
1 tsp mustard seeds
1 tbsp *chana dal*
1 tbsp *urad dal*
2 dry red chillies
Salt to taste

Wash *arbi* well to remove all residual mud and then half-cook it in a pressure cooker. After one whistle, switch off the cooker and let the pressure settle. Take out the *arbis*, wash in cold water, and remove the peel. Cut them into medium-sized pieces, put them in a bowl, and pour in a few spoons of sesame oil. Mix well, so they are all coated with the oil, and keep aside.

For the seasoning, dry roast *chana dal*, red chillies (broken in half), *urad dal*, and sesame seeds. Roast each ingredient separately as they roast at different speeds. Let them cool. Grind them to a coarse powder in the mixer-grinder, adding a pinch of asafoetida and salt to taste.

Heat a few tbsp of sesame oil in a frying pan, and add coriander seeds, mustard seeds, 1 tbsp of *chana dal*, 1 tbsp of *urad dal*, and 4 red chillies, broken in half. Once the mustard seeds begin to pop, add in the oiled *arbi* and a pinch of salt. Put a lid on the pan and let the *arbi* slow cook. Stir it every few minutes to make sure it does not stick to the base. Once it begins to cook, add in the fresh ground seasoning and let it cook till it is soft and begins to roast in parts. Once this happens, turn off the gas and let it cool.

Take the cooked and seasoned *arbi*, pat it by hand into cutlets, and coat each with semolina on either side. Heat cooking oil in a pan and shallow-fry the cutlets, flipping it over once each side is cooked. Wait for the semolina to brown and the outer layer of the cutlet to become crisp. Take them off the frying pan, and place on a tissue to pat off the excess oil.

Serve hot with chutney or dip.

Notes:
—This dish was discovered accidentally while we were cooking a meal in 1Shanthiroad as the *arbi* meant for a dry *sabzi* got overcooked and mushed. The resulting cutlets turned out better than the original plan.

Khandvi

Dimple B Shah

Serves 4

1 cup gram flour
3 cups sour curd
2½ cups water
1 tsp ginger paste
½ tsp green chilli paste
1 tsp turmeric powder
¼ tsp asafoetida
Salt to taste
1 sprig of coriander leaves
¼ cup grated coconut

TEMPERING:
1 tbsp oil
8–10 curry leaves
1 tsp mustard seeds
2 tsp white sesame seeds
2 green chillies

Add 2½ cups of water to sour curd and stir well. Add ginger paste, green chilli paste, turmeric powder, asafoetida, and salt. Add gram flour and whisk till it is well mixed, smooth, and has no lumps. Pour this batter in a saucepan or broad frying pan. Switch on the stove and keep the flame on low. Stir continuously for 15 to 20 minutes on low flame, till the batter is cooked (making sure no lumps are formed). The final consistency of the batter should be a little thicker than pancake or *dosa* batter.

Grease plates, trays, or *thalis* with oil. Finely chop coriander leaves, mix with grated coconut, and keep aside.

Test the batter by spreading a spoonful on the greased surface. Once it cools, use your thumb to lift and roll it from one side. If it rolls without sticking, the batter is ready. If it sticks or loses shape, cook for a few more minutes and test again. Once the batter is thickened to the right consistency, pour ½ to ⅔ cups of the batter on each of the greased plates. Spread thinly and evenly with a spatula. This step needs to be done quickly; if the batter is left in the pan it will thicken and be difficult to spread.

Allow the batter to cool and sprinkle the coriander and grated coconut mix. Use a knife to cut the sheets into strips of equal size (about 2 inches wide), and roll them with your thumb starting from one end. Place these rolls on a plate.

For tempering, heat oil in a tempering spoon and add mustard seeds. Once they splutter, add curry leaves, finely-chopped green chillies, and sesame seeds. Fry for a few seconds and add this hot onto the *khandvi* rolls.

Serve as a snack with coriander chutney or coriander-mint chutney.

Notes:
—If the curd is not sour, add the juice of ½ a lime to it.

—The coriander-coconut mixture can be used as garnish instead of as a stuffing if you prefer, along with the tempering.

—*Khandvi*, also known as *patuli* or *suralichi vadi*, is a popular savoury, healthy snack in Maharashtrian as well as Gujarati cuisine.

Potato Mustard Baked Chips

Suresh Jayaram

Serves 6–8

6 medium-sized potatoes
4 tbsp mustard seed paste
4 tbsp cooking oil
Salt to taste

Cut potatoes into thick slices, keeping the skin on. Boil the slices in water with salt till they are *al dente*.

Preheat the oven to 90 degrees Celsius. Grease a baking tray with oil and evenly lay potato slices on the tray. Smear the slices with mustard seed paste and bake for 20 minutes.

Serve hot.

Notes:
—An easy option is to use *kasundi* (a Bengali mustard seed relish) as a substitute for mustard seed paste.

SOUPS
AND
SALADS

Zucchini and Pea Soup with Basil ✦ Beetroot Soup ✦ Kosambari ✦ Welcome to Paradise ✦ Half-Moon in the Forest Salad ✦ Pikachu Salad

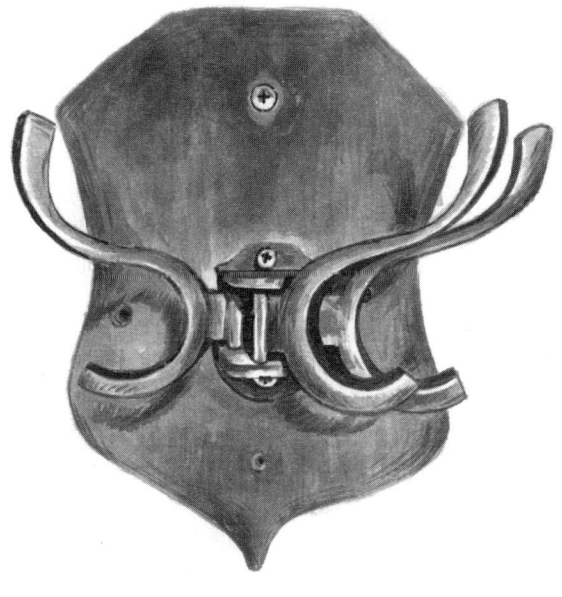

Zucchini and Pea Soup with Basil

Thomas & Renée Rapedius

Serves 8

5 tbsp olive oil
1 bulb of garlic
6 green zucchinis
1 l vegetable broth
500 ml water
500 g frozen peas
50 g basil leaves
200 g feta
1 tsp lemon zest
Salt to taste
Black pepper powder to taste

Separate and peel cloves of garlic; cut zucchini into 3-cm-thick slices. Crumble feta into 1 cm to 2 cm pieces.

Heat oil in a very large saucepan over medium to high temperature. Add whole garlic cloves and fry for 2 to 3 minutes until they turn golden in color, stirring constantly. Add zucchini with 2 tsp of salt and plenty of pepper. Fry for 3 minutes, stirring constantly. Pour in vegetable broth and 500 ml of water and bring to a boil over high heat. Reduce flame and let the soup cook for 7 minutes, until the zucchini is soft but still green. Add frozen peas. Stir for 1 minute, then add basil to the saucepan. Remove soup from the heat and purée with a hand blender or in a mixer-grinder until smooth and bright green.

To serve, divide the soup into bowls and garnish with crumbled feta and lemon zest. Finally, season with a strong pinch of pepper and drizzle with a little olive oil.

Beetroot Soup

Ayisha Abraham

Serves 2

1 small onion
3–4 beetroots
2–3 cloves of garlic
1-inch piece of ginger
1–2 tbsp butter
1–2 tbsp olive oil
2 cups vegetable stock
Salt to taste
Black pepper powder to taste

GARNISH:
A few spoons of curd
4–5 basil leaves

Finely chop onion and ginger. Peel and chop beetroots into large chunks. In a pan, heat butter and olive oil, and sauté onions with garlic cloves and ginger. Add vegetable stock and chopped beetroots. Boil till beetroots are well cooked and soft enough to be blended (you can pressure cook them as well, giving it one or two whistles). Cool it down and blend till puréed in a mixer-grinder. Add salt and pepper, and boil again before serving.

Serve hot; dish into soup bowls and add a dollop of homemade curd and finely-chopped homegrown basil to give it colour.

Notes:
—The vegetable stock can be either water boiled with vegetables like carrots, beans, or leeks for example, or a soup cube dissolved in a cup of water.

—This beetroot soup was my father's favourite dinnertime recipe. He loved to cook what he had tasted on his travels, and this borscht variation was one such dish. Variations of this recipe have lasted three generations in the family, since my father first made us sample it as a dish he remembered and loved from a visit to Poland. Originally Ukrainian, it is a common soup across East Europe. It is comfort food for our long evenings in Bangalore, especially on a chilly and windy evening when a hot soup nourishes the soul.

Kosambari

NS Harsha

Serves 2

½ cup *moong dal*
1 cup chopped cucumber
2 tbsp grated carrot
1 tbsp finely-chopped coriander leaves
2 tbsp grated coconut
½ lime
1 green chilli
Salt to taste

TEMPERING:
2 tbsp oil
½ tsp mustard seeds
A pinch of asafoetida
1 dry red chilli
5–6 curry leaves

Soak *moong dal* in water for an hour. Wash in running water, strain, and put in a salad bowl. Add cucumber, carrot, coriander leaves, and grated coconut. Squeeze half a lime on top and mix well.

If you like a tinge of heat, either add 1 small finely-chopped chilli directly into the salad or soak the chopped chilli in 1 tbsp of water for a few minutes then sprinkle that chilli-water onto the salad so as to avoid chewing on chilli directly.

In a pan, heat oil and add mustard seeds. Once they splutter, add a pinch of asafoetida and switch off the stove. Now, add red chilli broken in half and 5 to 6 curry leaves. Wait for a couple of minutes and add to the salad.

Add salt as per taste, mix well and serve immediately.

Notes:
—This recipe has been previously published in the Artists Cookbook by Mori Art Museum (MAM) in 2020.

—The recipe is in collaboration with my mother—Chandrika MN.

Welcome to Paradise

Barblina Meierhans

Serves 2

SALAD:
4 carrots
2 apples
1 cup fresh coriander leaves
1 fresh red chilli

DRESSING:
3 tbsp apple cider vinegar
3 tbsp rapeseed oil
1 tsp honey
A pinch of ground black peppercorns
A pinch of salt

Pour vinegar in a small bowl, add honey, ground peppercorns, and a pinch of salt. Stir well, till honey and vinegar are well mixed. Add rapeseed oil and mix again, till the dressing has the desired consistency.

Peel and grate carrots into a bowl. Cut red chilli in half lengthwise, chop into small pieces, and add to the bowl. Cut apples into quarters, remove the seeds, and grate them into the bowl. Add dressing immediately (so as to not let the apples oxidise and turn brown) and stir gently. Keep aside 3 to 6 whole coriander leaves, chop the rest into halves, and add to the salad. Stir carefully.

If serving as a side dish, put the whole coriander leaves as a decoration in the middle of the salad. If serving as a main dish, serve the salad on two plates, put 3 coriander leaves as decoration in the middle of each plate and serve with cheese *naan* or garlic *naan*. *Bon appetit!*

Notes:
—Choose an apple with a slightly tart flavour, like Gravenstein.

—Apple cider vinegar can be replaced with similar, slightly sweet vinegars.

—If you want to reduce the spice, remove the seeds of the chilli before you cut it into pieces.

—As a side dish, it can be served with rice/*dal*/spinach, with a vegetarian *thali*, with *chäschnöpfli* (cheese nubs), or some kind of cheesy Swiss noodles.

—Serving option without wheat: instead of serving with bread or *naan*, you can add some flax seeds to the salad, or garnish it with roasted sunflower seeds.

—This dish is 100% experimental, just invented. It's inspired by the impressive residency time at 1Shanthiroad and by the manner in which a good friend likes to eat apples.

Half-Moon in the Forest Salad

Ankit Ravani

Serves 2

2 tbsp olive oil
2 cloves of garlic
½ tbsp sesame seeds
2 long green brinjals
1 radish
1 capsicum
10–15 leaves of spinach
8–9 green olives
4–5 walnuts
½ tbsp sunflower seeds
½ tbsp pumpkin seeds
4 slices of bread
Salt to taste

DRESSING:
1 ½ tbsp lime juice
3 tbsp olive oil
1 tbsp olive brine
1 tsp coconut oil
5 basil leaves
2 cloves of garlic
Zest of ½ a lime
½ tsp crushed black peppercorns
Salt to taste

GARNISH:
10 basil leaves
4–6 dried figs

Blanch spinach leaves and chop in half. Chop radish into thin semicircular pieces (half-moons), brinjal into thick discs, olives in half, half-julienne the capsicum, mince the garlic, and chop figs. Keep all of these separately.

Heat 2 tbsp olive oil in a pan. Add half the minced garlic, a dash of crushed pepper, and sesame seeds into the hot oil and let them sizzle. Place brinjal discs to toast in the pan. Sprinkle salt, cover, and cook. Flip them and toast till they are brown on both sides.

Toast the walnuts, pumpkin, and sunflower seeds in another pan till they develop some colour. Break the walnuts into chunks once they cool.

For the dressing, in a bowl add 1½ tbsp lime juice, 2 to 3 tbsp olive oil, 1 tbsp olive brine, 1 tsp coconut oil, 4 to 5 leaves of chopped basil, the remaining minced garlic, zest of half a lime, ½ tsp crushed peppercorns, and salt to taste. Mix this vigorously and let it rest.

Toss all the ingredients along with the dressing in a large bowl, keeping aside a few of the radish half-moons. Toast bread until reddish brown and tear into small chunks. Add the crunchy bread chunks last and toss again.

Serve the salad garnished with torn basil, some of the radish half-moons, and chopped figs.

Pikachu Salad

Benjamin Buchanan

Serves 2

1 cucumber
½ red onion
3 tomatoes
1 bunch of mint leaves
½ cup roasted peanuts
3 green chillies

DRESSING:
2 tbsp soy sauce
1 lemon
Splash of vinegar

Finely slice onion and green chillies, halve tomatoes and then cut into quarters. Partially peel cucumber (in alternating stripes), keep it whole and slice at an angle. Combine these in a bowl, along with peanuts and mint leaves. Add a good glug of soy sauce and the juice of 1 lemon with a splash of vinegar. These will start to break down the tomato a bit, bring out the juice, and soften things up.

Garnish with finely-sliced mint leaves and roasted peanuts, toss and serve.

Notes:
—This is a great side dish with BBQ or as a salad on its own. Adding puréed roasted garlic to the dressing is a good idea.

—Telegraph cucumbers are pretty common in New Zealand and are of a decent size, so you might need more than 1 cucumber depending on what you have access to. The cucumber and peanuts are the stars of the dish.

—For a time I was working in a small dumpling factory. One of my daily chores was to produce three salads for the shop counter, two of which were the same every day, and a third one I could just make up. This was the only opportunity for any creativity in the job, and I tried to replicate a cucumber and peanut side dish I had in China, having spent 3 months there on residency through the Asia New Zealand Foundation (the same people who supported my visit to 1Shanthiroad). I made up a bunch of salads during that time and this is the best. Hope it works for you, *aroha nui*.

MAINS

Spanish Paella ✦ Stir-fried Veggies with Pasta ✦ Pasta with Sausage, Basil, and Mustard Sauce ✦ Capellini with Tomato Pesto ✦ Stuffed Capsicum Bake ✦ Christmas Nut Roast ✦ Azerbaijan Stuffed Spiral Bread ✦ Ratatouille ✦ Roast Beef with Mashed Potatoes and Sauerkraut ✦ Beef Tongue with Olives ✦ Mutton Thalki ✦ Kashmiri Yakhni ✦ Khichra ✦ Chemmeen Roast ✦ Kozhi Ularthiyathu ✦ Undhiyo ✦ Litti Chokha

Spanish Paella

Ricardo Gallego

Serves 15

8 cups rice
17 cups vegetable/chicken/seafood broth
6 piquillo peppers
800 g chicken (curry cut with skin)
1 big onion
3 cloves of garlic
250 g French beans
250 g lima butter beans
4 artichokes
Salt to taste
Black pepper powder to taste
Rosemary to taste
5 threads of saffron
1 cup extra virgin olive oil

Finely chop onions and garlic. Chop French beans into inch-long pieces. Cut piquillo peppers into strips and roast them. Keep aside.

Heat 2 tbsp extra virgin olive oil in a wide, flat-bottomed pan over medium heat. Then add chicken pieces and brown on both sides. Transfer chicken to a plate. Add finely-chopped onions and garlic to the pan, and cook until soft and translucent (for 4 to 5 minutes). Add French beans and lima beans, and cook for a couple more minutes. Add the rice, stir, and toast for 3 to 4 minutes, adding in a little more oil if needed. Add salt and pepper to taste. Pour the broth into the pan and shake the pan so the rice is evenly distributed. Then remember the only rule—do not stir the rice again!

Take a few threads of saffron and toast them very lightly. For this, place the saffron in a piece of aluminium foil and fold it like an envelope. Apply a little bit of heat with a lighter (just for 3 seconds) and add the toasted saffron to the pan—it will tint the rice to a characteristic yellow.

Once the mixture begins to bubble, place the chicken pieces and artichokes in the pan; then place some strips of piquillo peppers and rosemary on top. Since you cannot stir, place every ingredient in the position you want them to appear in the finished dish. Simmer over low to medium heat for about 20 minutes (or until the rice is done), rotating the pan as needed to cook the rice towards the edges. You can increase the heat for the last few minutes of the cooking process to further caramelize the *socarrat* (the crispy golden-brown bottom). Turn off the heat and cover with a cotton cloth for 5 to 10 minutes. And *voilà!*

Each person can take a wooden spoon and eat directly from the pan, starting from the rim and going towards the centre where the wonderful *socarrat* lies.

Notes:
—The variety of rice used for *paella* is called *bomba* rice, commonly available in Spain, but any rice that takes double the amount of water and around 20 minutes to cook will do.

—The broth must be a little more than double the quantity of rice—so you can adjust ratios according to the number of guests. If you are using chicken, then 100 g of chicken per person.

—Instead of piquillo peppers, capsicums can be used.

—*Paella* is a very versatile dish that accepts any variation on ingredients, yet one rule must always be followed, and that is NOT TO STIR THE RICE, because it is the secret behind the distinct flavour of *paella*. By not stirring, the bottom layer of rice will toast and caramelize, yielding the *socarrat*—the tastiest part of the *paella*.

—*Paella* holds a special place in Spanish cuisine and culture. It is a dish that is usually cooked on Sundays when the whole family can sit together and spend some quality time enjoying a dish made to share. It is made in a large pan, *'paellera'*, that doubles as a serving plate for everybody to dig in with their spoons in the same plate. Bonding over a *paella* is a familial ritual in gatherings.

—This *paella* recipe is a very traditional one that combines chicken with vegetables, and blends the humble rice with the royal Spanish saffron.

—It is a humble dish, just rice with assorted ingredients like vegetables, meat, or seafood. It is very nourishing, served without pretension, and appropriate for 1Shanthiroad events in which people bond over art and food.

Stir-fried Veggies with Pasta

Ashok Vish

Serves 4

500 g wide pasta (such as fettuccine)
2 tbsp olive or vegetable oil
1 tbsp ginger-garlic paste
½ onion
1 red capsicum
250 g mushrooms
150 g broccoli
1 tbsp soy sauce
1 tbsp hoisin sauce
1 tbsp rice wine vinegar
1 tbsp sesame oil
1 tsp honey
Salt to taste

Start by cooking pasta in boiling water until *al dente,* with salt in the water. Drain the pasta and immediately run cold water over it; set aside.

Chop onions, red capsicum, mushrooms, and broccoli. In a large thick pan, heat olive or vegetable oil over low heat and add ginger-garlic paste. Add onions, red capsicum, mushrooms, and broccoli, and continue to stir. Let the vegetables cook and add salt to taste. While they cook, mix together soy sauce, hoisin sauce, rice wine vinegar, sesame oil, and a dash of honey. Adjust these ingredients according to your preferred taste. Once the vegetables are cooked, add the mixed sauce into the skillet and stir until the vegetables are coated. Finally, add in the pasta.

Serve with Sriracha sauce on the side.

Pasta with Sausage, Basil, and Mustard Sauce

Ashok Vish

Serves 6–8

500 g penne, rigatoni, or medium shell pasta
1 tbsp extra-virgin olive oil
650 g of Italian sausages
¾ cup dry white wine
¾ cup heavy cream
3 tbsp mustard sauce
2 dry red chillies
1 cup basil leaves
Salt to taste

Start by cooking pasta in boiling water until *al dente,* with salt in the water. Drain the pasta and immediately run cold water over it; set aside.

Remove meat from the sausage casings and crumble. Crush red chillies and thinly slice basil leaves. Heat olive oil in a large, deep skillet. Add sausage meat and brown it over moderately high heat for about 5 minutes. Add wine and simmer, scraping up the browned bits from the bottom, until the liquid is reduced by half (it will take about 5 minutes). Add cream, mustard sauce, and crushed red chillies and simmer for 2 minutes. Remove from heat and add the pasta and basil. Toss the preparation to coat evenly.

Serve immediately.

Capellini with Tomato Pesto

Julia D Kjelgaard

Serves 4

450 g capellini

PESTO:
⅓ cup pine nuts
170 g canned tomato paste
½ cup fresh parsley leaves
¼ cup basil leaves
½ cup olive oil
½ cup grated parmesan cheese
2 cloves of garlic
½ tsp salt
Freshly ground black peppercorns to taste

Lightly toast pine nuts in an oven at 170 degrees Celsius (or in a skillet) until golden. Finely chop parsley, basil, and garlic. To make the pesto, combine pine nuts with all the remaining ingredients for the sauce in a medium bowl.

Bring a 6 litre pot of water to a boil. Add the pasta and cook until *al dente*. Before draining the pasta, beat 2 tbsp of the boiling pasta water into the sauce. Drain the pasta and return it to the pot or transfer it into a large bowl. Spoon on the sauce and toss quickly.

Serve immediately.

Notes:
—Fresh basil can be replaced with dried basil, based on availability.

—Capellini can be replaced with vermicelli or spaghetti.

—The pesto can be made up to 24 hours in advance, covered, and chilled. Bring to room temperature before mixing it with the pasta. You can also make a double batch and freeze half.

—This pesto can be put on any kind of pasta or in anything else you think might be good—cauliflower, eggplant, lasagna, etc.

—Add more water or oil if you like the pesto thinner.

—I usually use small pine nuts that are imported from China which do not need to be ground. If you are using the longer ones, then break them into half after toasting.

—Pine nuts can be replaced with chopped walnuts, cashews, or pumpkin seeds.

Stuffed Capsicum Bake

Suresh Jayaram

Serves 12–15

10 large green capsicums
6 large potatoes
100 g mozzarella cheese
2 large carrots
100 g green peas
100 g sweet corn
1 cup cooked rice
1 tbsp black pepper powder
1 tbsp dried oregano
1 tbsp dried thyme
2 tbsp cooking oil
Salt to taste

Boil potatoes till they are well cooked. Cool, peel, and mash well. Dice carrots and boil them with peas in water till they are tender; drain. Mix the boiled carrots, peas, and sweet corn kernels into the mashed potato. Add pepper, oregano, thyme, and salt to taste.

Cut capsicums horizontally in half, giving you 2 cup-shaped pieces to fill the mixture into; trim the stalk so it is flush with the top. Stuff the capsicum halves with the mashed potato mixture till just below the rim, then add a spoonful of rice, and top it with a layer of grated mozzarella cheese.

Grease a baking pan with cooking oil and place the stuffed capsicum halves on it. Preheat the oven to 90 degrees Celsius and bake the stuffed capsicum for about 20 minutes until the cheese on top melts.

Serve with dip or chutney.

Notes:
—Mozzarella cheese can be replaced with paneer if that is preferred.

Christmas Nut Roast

George Demir & Tim Wolfgarten

Serves 6

250 g mushrooms
2 onions
8 cloves of garlic
1 capsicum
3 carrots
1 radish
1 cup tomato paste
3 bundles of mixed herbs (rosemary, thyme, oregano)
200 g split red lentils (*masoor dal*)
1 cup vegetable stock
300 g chopped bread
500 g mixed nuts (almonds, walnuts, cashews, etc.)
1 tbsp mustard oil
200 g cheddar cheese
6 eggs
All-purpose flour as required
1 tbsp mustard seed paste
Salt to taste
Crushed black peppercorns to taste

Grate carrots and radish. Finely chop all other vegetables, herbs, and garlic. Stir-fry mushrooms, 1 chopped onion, and 3 cloves of garlic with salt and pepper and keep aside. Separately stir-fry the second onion, the leftover garlic, capsicum, carrots, and radish. When cooked, add in the finely-chopped herbs. Keep aside.

In a large pot, cook lentils in vegetable stock. Grind the nuts roughly and stir-fry with chopped bread in mustard oil.

Mix all of the above and add grated cheddar, eggs, a bit of flour, tomato paste, and mustard paste. Adjust salt. Spread the mixture in a shallow greased dish and place it in the oven at 200 degrees Celsius, covered with aluminium foil, for 30 minutes. Remove the foil and bake for another 20 minutes.

Let it cool and serve as small cut pieces.

Azerbaijan Stuffed Spiral Bread

Arundhati Ghosh

Serves 4

BREAD:
1½ cups all-purpose flour
½ cup milk
1 tbsp yeast
¼ tsp baking powder
1 tsp sugar
½ tsp salt
2 eggs
1 tbsp oil
1 tbsp butter
3 tsp white sesame seeds
3 tsp nigella seeds

FILLING:
150 g beef or mutton *kheema*
1 tbsp oil
1 medium onion
6 cloves of garlic
2 green chillies
2 tbsp tomato ketchup
1 tsp soy sauce
Salt to taste
1 tsp any herb you like
1 tbsp all-purpose flour
50–60 g broken cheddar cheese

Sift flour, salt, and baking powder. In a separate bowl, slightly warm the milk, add sugar, and mix. Add yeast and let it bloom for 5 to 10 minutes. When frothy, it is ready.

Whisk 1 egg with oil and butter. Add yeast mix and egg mix to the flour and knead for 10 minutes. The final dough must be smooth but not too sticky. Cover and leave to rise for 60 to 90 minutes (or till it doubles).

While the dough is rising, make the filling. Heat 1 tbsp of oil in a pan and add finely-chopped onion, cloves of garlic, and green chillies. Wait for the onions to start browning on the edges and then add *kheema*. Stir the mix and fry. Add tomato ketchup, soy sauce, salt, and herbs. Don't over-stir; just once every couple of minutes till the meat is browned enough. Add 1 tbsp of flour and mix it all in. Flour absorbs the extra liquid and thickens the mixture. Keep aside.

Roll the dough out to a ¼-inch thick rectangle. Then cut into strips of about 1 to 1½ inch width. You should get about 3 strips. Don't make them too thin because they will be difficult to fill. Spoon the *kheema* filling and broken cheese along the middle of each strip. Bring the edges together and pinch it close to make a long rope. Wet your fingers and pinch the edges firmly to ensure it is sealed well; else the cheese will melt and ooze out during baking. Repeat with all the strips.

On a baking mat or baking tray lined with a parchment, coil the ropes into a spiral starting from the centre. When one rope ends, attach the next rope to it so as to continue the circle. You can make one big spiral or two small spirals with this quantity. Leave covered to rise for another 30 minutes.

Whisk 1 egg in a bowl. With a brush paint the bread with the egg wash and sprinkle nigella seeds and white sesame seeds. Bake in a preheated oven at 200 degrees Celsius for 30 to 35 minutes (or till nice and golden-brown on the top). Take out from the oven and cool on the rack.

Serve warm, cut into triangles like cake or broken into ropes.

Notes:
—The all-purpose flour can be replaced with half all-purpose flour and half whole wheat flour.

—Beef or mutton *kheema* is used for best results, but for vegetarians, cheese with fried onion, capsicum, tomato, or paneer will also be good.

—This is a filling snack and does not need anything else with it. It lasts up to 3 days if stored in the refrigerator.

—This bread is from Azerbaijan, and was taught to me by my friend and baking teacher Kalika Bali.

Ratatouille

Birte Hendricks

Serves 6

Olive oil as required
1 tbsp sugar
2–3 cloves of garlic
1 onion
2 brinjals
10–12 tomatoes
1 tbsp parsley leaves
1 tsp basil leaves
1 tsp dried oregano
A dash of black pepper powder
A dash of salt

Finely chop onion and garlic. Cut brinjal into medium-sized chunks. Cut 5 to 6 tomatoes into quarters and blend the rest.

Heat olive oil in a large skillet and stir in the onion. Add sugar to the onions and let it caramelise. Add in brinjals and roast the chunks for a few minutes. The brinjal will absorb the olive oil—add more if required. Make sure the brinjal isn't dry, otherwise it will turn black very quickly. Add garlic and tomatoes (both the cut pieces and the blended portion). Add salt, basil, parsley, black pepper powder, and oregano, and mix well. Simmer on a low flame, until the vegetables are soft, for about 30 minutes. Adjust the fresh herbs to taste and let the ratatouille rest for some time.

Decorate with some basil leaves and serve hot or cold, as a main or side dish— everything is possible with ratatouille.

Roast Beef with Mashed Potatoes and Sauerkraut

Uwe Jonas

Serves 10

3 kg slab of beef
Salt and pepper to taste

REMOULADE:
600 ml sunflower or vegetable oil
4 egg yolks
2 tbsp sugar
2 tbsp vinegar
2 tbsp mustard sauce
2 tbsp lime juice
8 small gherkins
1 small onion
2 tbsp capers
2 tbsp parsley leaves
2 tbsp dried tarragon
2 tsp dill leaves
2 tbsp crème fraîche (or sour cream)
100 g yogurt
2 tsp salt

MASHED POTATOES:
1 kg potatoes
120 ml milk
80 g butter
A pinch of nutmeg powder
Salt to taste

CARAMELIZED SAUERKRAUT WITH TOMATO PURÉE:
1 kg sauerkraut
2 tbsp oil
3 tbsp sugar
200 g tomato purée

Wash and clean the cut of beef, season it with salt and pepper, and quickly braise it on all sides in a hot pan. Then, place it on an oven rack, position a tray underneath to collect any fat, and leave in the oven for 7 to 8 hours at 80 to 100 degrees Celsius. Make sure to check the temperature regularly and turn down the oven if this core temperature has been reached. An important tool here is a meat thermometer that measures the temperature at the centre of the cut of meat. This temperature must not exceed 56 degrees Celsius for longer periods to ensure the meat remains pinkish in colour. Check the temperature regularly and turn down the oven if the core temperature has been reached.

While the beef cooks, you can start on the remoulade. For this, beat egg yolks, sugar, vinegar, mustard sauce, and lime juice with a hand blender at an intermediate setting until a thick consistency is achieved (3 to 5 minutes). Slowly add oil, little by little, and mix it into the mixture. Do not add too much oil at once as the mixture will curdle. Add salt. The mixture that results is a tasty mayonnaise! Now finely chop gherkins, onion, and capers and mix them into the mayonnaise, along with the herbs. Finally, mix in yoghurt and crème fraîche and the remoulade is now finished!

For the mashed potatoes, peel and cook potatoes in salted water. Once cooked, drain the water and mash with milk, butter, salt, and a little nutmeg. Mash until a light, dough-like consistency is achieved.

For caramelized sauerkraut, first thoroughly wash the sauerkraut. Add oil and sugar to a pot and stir until the sugar has dissolved. Now add in the drained sauerkraut and concentrated tomato purée. Keep the heat on and stir regularly until a slightly reddish colour is achieved.

Slice the roast beef and serve while reasonably warm, accompanied by mashed potatoes and caramelized sauerkraut.

Notes:
—Sauerkraut is white cabbage leaves, pickled in vinegar.

—This is a dish that I generally prepare in summertime for the monthly dinner parties at Lichtenberg Studios and sometimes also for the alumni meetings of the Goethe-Institut's bangaloREsidency.

—To me, roast beef is primarily a dish served in the UK or USA, but it does not have such a prominent position

in German cuisine. It was more popular in Germany in the 1970s, back when people invited more friends over and there were more parties that often involved a lot of alcohol. Large amounts of food, often including fatty dishes, were served on such occasions in order to provide a solid foundation in people's stomachs for drinking. Moreover, the advantage of roast beef is that it can also be eaten cold or when it is still slightly warm. Nowadays however, this dish is rarely prepared: firstly, a large piece of meat is required, which only makes sense with eight or more guests, and, secondly, remoulade is almost obligatory with this dish and a lot of people don't like remoulade. I have often watched people eating a thin slice of roast beef without any of the homemade remoulade and this doesn't taste half as good, and is a sacrilege in my opinion.

—All in all, this is a perfect dish to be served at Lichtenberg Studios and many residents from our exchange with 1Shanthiroad have eaten this with great delight—it is easy to prepare, has a lot of history, great scope for interpretation, and many references to (eating) habits in Germany that have changed over the years.

Beef Tongue with Olives

Janet Meaney

Serves 4

1 ox tongue
1 onion
1 carrot
3 stalks of celery
8 potatoes
8 cloves
3 bay leaves
10 black peppercorns
1 tsp salt
16 olives

VINAIGRETTE:
¼ cup olive oil
1 tbsp Dijon mustard
½ cup red wine vinegar
1 tbsp black peppercorns

Wash tongue in cold water and place in a pot. Cover it with water. Add onion and carrot cut in quarters, celery cut in halves, whole potatoes, cloves, bay leaves, peppercorns, and salt. Bring the water to a quick boil on high heat, then lower the heat, cover, and simmer for 1½ hours. Remove the tongue; let it sit for 5 minutes, then peel it and slice diagonally. Place it on a platter with the carrots, potatoes, celery, and olives.

For the vinaigrette, beat together olive oil, Dijon mustard, red wine vinegar, and freshly ground peppercorns. Drizzle the vinaigrette along the length of the tongue and serve.

Notes:
—Tongue was often cooked by my mother despite the stigma attached to it as a food of the poor, discarded by the rich because of what it was. In performance, I see this as a mind-set looking for a challenge.

Mutton Thalki

(Mutton Stir-fry)

Miya Shivaram

Serves 4–6

1 kg mutton
25–30 Guntur red chillies
2 tbsp cumin seeds
1 tbsp turmeric powder
5 tbsp oil
Salt to taste
1 sprig of curry leaves

Cut mutton into curry-sized pieces and marinate in turmeric powder and salt for 30 minutes. Heat oil in a thick-bottomed pot and add cumin seeds. When it splutters, add mutton. Sauté and cook for 15 minutes. Add in whole red chillies, stir well, and cook until the mutton is well done. Check for seasoning and serve garnished with curry leaves.

Serve with *pulao*, rice, *chapati*, or *poori*.

Notes:
—*Thalki* can be translated to mean stir-fry pot. This recipe is a specialty of the transgender community in Bangalore and is recommended as nutritious for those undergoing sex change operations. This dish requires very few ingredients and it acts as a whole meal—often without even rice. In the community, when the mother, daughter, *chela,* and *nathi chela* get together, they make this dish as the main course during functions.

—The use of mutton comes from the fact that the transgender community most often associate themselves with Islamic traditions, which keeps them from consuming pork. That, combined with the fact that chicken produces too much heat in our bodies, makes mutton *thalki* a very frequently made dish within the community.

Kashmiri Yakhni

Ayisha Abraham

Serves 4–5

1 kg mutton chops
2–3 tbsp *ghee*
½ tsp asafoetida
5 cloves
4–5 pods of green cardamom
1 cinnamon stick
2–3 green chillies
2 bay leaves
3 tbsp fennel seeds
1 tsp dry ginger powder
1 tbsp cumin seeds
600 g curd
Salt to taste

Heat *ghee* in a pressure cooker and fry cardamom, cloves, bay leaves, and cinnamon. Add green chillies slit in half and a pinch of asafoetida. Add mutton chops and fry till the water starts drying up. Add an additional cup of water and pressure cook till the mutton is tender—roughly 20 to 30 minutes.

While the mutton is cooking, powder fennel seeds and cumin seeds in a mixer-grinder. Add dry ginger powder and salt. Mix this powder with curd and whisk till it becomes a smooth sauce. Once the cooker is cooled enough to open, add the curd mixture to the cooked mutton chops and simmer for about 5 minutes.

Serve hot with white rice.

Notes:
—When I was growing up in New Delhi's Defence Colony, our neighbours of a few doors away were an older Kashmiri couple. We called them Mama and Papa and we often visited their home where Mama ran a tailoring shop. In the afternoons after school, Mama would offer us this warm meal to tide over the hunger till it was dinner time. This *yakhni* and its associated aromas have become a memory of growing up.

Khichra

Jahangir Asgar Jani

Serves 6

1 kg mutton
3 tbsp ginger-garlic paste
4 tbsp red chilli powder
3 tsp salt
4 tsp coriander powder
1 tsp turmeric powder
1 cup chopped onions
1 cup curd
2 tsp allspice
1 cup oil
250 g pounded wheat
½ cup *chana dal*
¼ cup *toor dal*
¼ cup *moong dal*
¼ cup *masoor dal*
¼ cup *urad dal*

TEMPERING:
2 tbsp *ghee*
2 onions

GARNISH:
1 sprig of coriander leaves
3 green chillies
4 lime wedges

Soak pounded wheat overnight. Soak all *dals* together overnight and boil next morning until tender. Mash cooked *dals* and keep aside. Boil broken wheat in 8 cups of water until tender. Mash or blend with the *dals*. Chop mutton into 1-inch pieces and keep aside. Finely chop onions.

Heat oil in a *kadhai* and add ginger-garlic paste, chilli powder, salt, coriander powder, turmeric powder, and chopped onions. Add the chopped mutton and cook for 15 minutes. Add curd and continue cooking. Add sufficient water to cook the meat until tender. Then add the wheat and *dal* mixture and allspice. Cook for 15 minutes till it attains a porridge-like consistency.

For the tempering, heat 2 tbsp of *ghee* and add in onions cut into slivers. Add this to the *khichra*.

Serve garnished with coriander leaves, green chillies, and lime wedges, with a side of leavened bread or *khameer roti*.

Notes:
—*Khichra* is traditionally made on the 10th day of Muharram by the Bohra Shia Muslim community, in remembrance of the martyrdom of Imam Hussain, the Prophet Muhammad's grandson in Iraq.

Chemmeen Roast

(Prawn Roast)

Anna Mary Magdalene

Serves 4

500 g prawns
5 tbsp coconut oil
1 tsp turmeric powder
1 tsp black pepper powder
1½ tsp *garam masala*
3 onions
4 green chillies
10 curry leaves
4 tbsp ginger-garlic paste
1 tsp lime juice
Salt to taste
Red chilli powder to taste

In a bowl, marinate prawns with ½ tsp turmeric powder, a dash of chilli powder, 2 tbsp of ginger-garlic paste, and lime juice. Mix well and keep aside for 20 to 30 minutes. Finely chop onions and green chillies.

Place a pan over medium flame, heat oil and add onions, green chillies, curry leaves, and 2 tbsp ginger-garlic paste. Fry until the onions become golden-brown. Then add *garam masala*, ½ tsp turmeric powder, pepper, salt, and chilli powder as required. Cook for 5 minutes and then add ½ a glass of water, along with the marinated prawns. Cover the pan and cook for 10 minutes until dry.

Serve with *dosa*, *appam*, or rice.

Kozhi Ularthiyathu

(Dry Chicken Roast)

Shivaji Panikkar

Serves 8–9

1 kg chicken
4 onions
1 coconut
2 green chillies
A handful of curry leaves
3-inch piece of ginger
15–18 cloves of garlic
1 tbsp mustard seeds
2 tbsp coconut oil
Salt to taste

MASALA:
1 tbsp coconut oil
2 bay leaves
6–8 black peppercorns
5 pods of green cardamom
2 tbsp cumin seeds
20 g cinnamon sticks
6 cloves
5 tbsp coriander seeds
2 tbsp dry red Kashmiri chillies
A pinch of fenugreek seeds
2 tbsp turmeric powder
A handful of curry leaves

Fry the ingredients listed under *masala* in a pan with a little bit of oil for a few minutes. Allow it to cool and grind finely in a mixer-grinder. Keep aside.

Finely chop onions, coconut, green chillies, ginger, and garlic. Cut chicken into small pieces. Heat oil in a pan over a medium flame and fry onions and garlic until they become soft. Add chopped coconut and mustard seeds and fry. Add curry leaves and fry until it becomes light brown. Add in the ground *masala* and 2 cups of water, along with salt to taste. When this is boiling, add chicken and cover. Cook on a slow flame for about an hour. Stir every now and then, if needed, and add more water if required. Make sure that the chicken roast isn't burning. Remove after ensuring that the chicken is cooked and dry.

Serve as a side with rice, *dosa*, or *roti*.

Notes:
—This is a central Kerala (Alappuzha district) recipe that I have seen being made from my childhood at my home in Kavalam, Kuttanad. The recipe is very special since it is offered annually to the family ancestor (Velichappadu Ammavan) along with toddy and other dishes such as *vatta-appam*.

Undhiyo

Heena Pari

Serves 8

VEGETABLES:
1 cup hyacinth beans (Surti *papdi*)
½ cup green peas
½ cup shelled hyacinth beans (*val na dana*)
½ cup shelled fresh *toor* (*tuver na dana*)
5 medium-sized Surti brinjal
5 medium-sized potatoes
250 g sweet potato
250 g purple yam (Surti *kand*)
1 raw banana

GREEN MASALA:
½ cup peanut powder
3 tbsp coriander-cumin powder
1½ tbsp green chilli-ginger paste
½ cup chopped cloves of garlic or green garlic shoots
2 tbsp sesame seeds
¼ tsp turmeric powder
1 tbsp salt or as per taste
2 tbsp sugar
¼ tsp *garam masala*
¼ tsp baking soda
2 cups coriander leaves
¾ fresh coconut
3 tsp oil
2 tsp lime juice or as per taste

MUTHIA:
1 cup fenugreek leaves
¼ cup wheat flour
4 tbsp gram flour
2½ tbsp semolina
1 tsp green chilli-ginger paste
1 tsp ginger paste
1 tsp green garlic shoot paste
¼ tsp coriander-cumin powder
¼ tsp turmeric powder
1 tsp sugar

¾ tsp salt or as per taste
1 tsp sesame seeds
2 tsp oil
Extra oil for frying

SEASONING:
½ tsp mustard seeds
½ tsp cumin seeds
½ tsp carom seeds
¼ tsp asafoetida
¼ tsp turmeric powder
2 tbsp oil
1 tsp sugar
¼ tsp salt
A pinch of baking soda

GARNISH:
1 cup coriander leaves
½ cup grated fresh coconut

First prepare the green *masala*. Take a large mixing bowl and add washed and chopped green coriander leaves, grated coconut, followed by all the other ingredients listed under green *masala*, including the oil. Mix well using your hand. Check the salt and spice level, and keep aside.

Skin raw banana and yam. Chop sweet potatoes, yam, and raw banana into medium-sized pieces. Clean potatoes and brinjals. Make a cross slit on the long end of the potatoes and brinjals (deep enough to stuff the green *masala* in). Next, take the green *masala* and stuff it in, keeping some *masala* aside (½ cup) for later. Take the chopped sweet potato, raw banana, and purple yam on a large plate, coat these with the green *masala*, and set aside.

For the *muthia*, take a large bowl and mix all the dry *muthia* ingredients well with 2 tsp oil. Knead it into a dough. You can add ⅔ tsp of water to help it mix well. Once the dough is ready, take a little oil on your hands and make small balls out of the dough. They should be the size of small limes but slightly oblong. Heat oil for frying to medium high. Deep-fry a few at a time till they are golden-brown. The *muthias* are ready and should be kept aside.

Take a large pressure cooker and heat oil for seasoning. Add mustard seeds, cumin seeds, and carom seeds and once they splutter, add turmeric powder and asafoetida. Add Surti *papdi*, green peas, fresh *tuver na dana,* and *val na dana*. Add a pinch of soda, salt, sugar, and ½ cup water to this. Close the cooker lid without the whistle and cook on medium heat for 5 minutes or till it begins to steam. Lower the heat, open the lid carefully, and mix the beans once. Then layer brinjal and potato on top of the beans. Sprinkle ¼ cup of green *masala* on top of this. Then add yam, sweet potato, and raw banana and sprinkle the remaining green *masala*. Close the cooker lid and let it cook for 15 to 20 minutes. Open the lid and mix it lightly. Add the extra oil from frying the *muthias* into the *undhiyo*. The methi flavoured oil will add to the *masala* and vegetables. Close the cooker lid and cook for another 15 minutes or till the vegetables are cooked. The smell of the *undhiyo* will also get flavourful once the vegetables are all cooked.

Open the lid of the cooker carefully, add the fried *muthias,* and mix gently so as not to break apart the vegetables. Cover the lid and cook for another 5 minutes. Cool to room temperature (for at least 2 hours) to incorporate the *masalas* well and for the *muthias* to soak up excess water/gravy.

Serve with fresh grated coconut and green coriander on top. Enjoy it as is or with *poori* and *shrikhand* on the side.

Notes:
—Old potatoes are matured and have a lighter skin; they work well for this recipe.

—The *muthias* are a great snack by themselves. They can be prepared a day before and stored in an airtight container once cooled.

—*Undhiyo* is a winter speciality and this version was made in our home by my grandmother, who is from the Surat region. It is a vegetarian delight using fresh green vegetables that are available during winter in Gujarat. I get vegetables from Surat/Mumbai to make this as I feel the *undhiyo* has a distinct taste with the vegetables from that region. Also some of the vegetables are specific to the region and not available easily elsewhere. (I have taken help from friends who travel often to get this for me. It is also possible to get the vegetables through courier.)

—This recipe involves a little time, so start the process very early if you need it ready for lunch. Or you can start mid-morning and have it for an early dinner. The preparation takes most of the time; the cooking process is relatively faster once the prep is in place. Involve household members or friends to speed up the process. I have worked with the ladies of my apartment community and made *undhiyo* for up to 80 people. With many hands working, it is a fun, joyous, and super delicious bonding event.

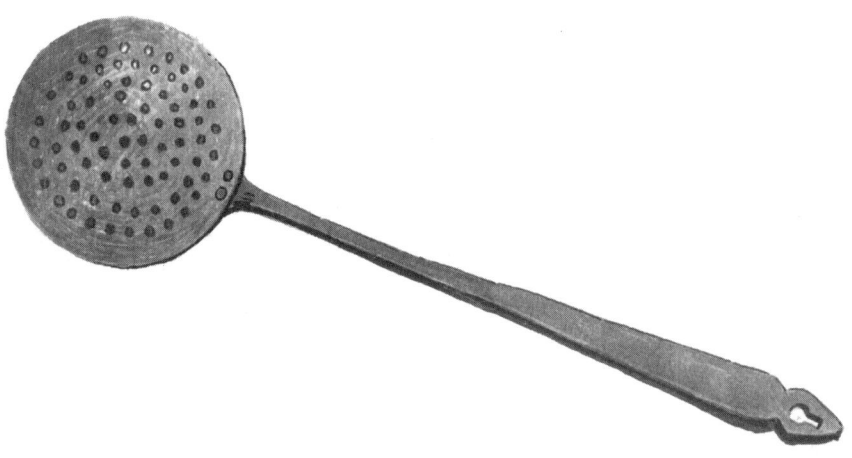

Litti Chokha

Shubham Kumar

Serves 4

LITTI DOUGH:
300 g wheat flour
¼ tsp salt
1 tbsp mustard oil
1 cup water

LITTI FILLING:
½ tsp cumin seeds
½ tsp fennel seeds
1 cup fried gram flour (*sattu*)
½ tsp carom seeds
½ tsp nigella seeds
½ tsp red chilli powder
2 green chillies
1-inch piece of ginger
3 cloves of garlic
½ small onion
1 sprig of coriander leaves
¼ tsp black salt
2 tsp lime juice
Salt to taste
2 tsp mustard oil
2 tbsp water
Refined vegetable oil for frying

CHOKHA:
300 g large brinjals
250 g tomatoes
3 green chillies
2 medium-sized onions
8 cloves of garlic
A few sprigs of coriander leaves
2 tbsp mustard oil
2 dry red chillies
Salt to taste

For the *litti*, take 250 g wheat flour, salt, and mustard oil in a bowl and add ¾ cup of water, little by little, kneading it constantly till the dough is soft. Add another ¼ cup water if it seems too dry. Cover and keep aside for 30 minutes.

For the *litti* filling, take 1 cup fried gram flour in a mixing bowl or pan. Add carom seeds, nigella seeds, red chilli powder, black salt, and lime juice. Coarsely crush cumin seeds and fennel seeds in a mortar and pestle and add to the mixture. Then finely chop and add green chillies, ginger, garlic, onion, and coriander. Lastly, add mustard oil and salt to taste. Sprinkle 1 to 2 tbsp of water and mix evenly. Add a little more water if required. If the fried gram flour filling is too dry, it can be felt when the *litti* is eaten. Test the moistness of the filling by taking 2 tbsp of the mix and pressing it into a ball in your fist. Once you open the fist, the mix should hold shape but disintegrate at the slightest pressure.

Divide the *litti* dough into golf-ball-sized balls. Sprinkle a little dry flour and roll into discs (5 to 6 inches in diameter) using a rolling pin. Place 2 tbsp of the filling in the centre and pleat and join the edges. Lightly roll the stuffed dough balls in your palms to get a round shape and keep aside.

Heat refined vegetable oil in a deep *kadhai* and deep-fry the *littis* on medium flame till the outer flour layer is brown. Check the first one you fry to see if the outer layer is cooked well.

To make the *chokha*, make two vertical cuts into the brinjals in a straight line. Pour some oil over the brinjal and the uncut tomato. Roast the brinjal and tomato on a high open flame, using a knife to check progress. Once cooked, remove from the flame and keep aside to cool. Once the brinjal and tomato are cooled, peel off their skin and transfer the flesh into a big bowl. To this, add finely-chopped green chillies and mash gently. Finely chop onion, garlic, and coriander leaves and add to the mix. Top with mustard oil and add salt to taste. Finally, burn 2 red chillies, finely chop them, and mix well with the preparation.

Serve by breaking open the *litti* and pouring *ghee* over it, along with the brinjal *chokha*.

Notes:
—Make sure the outer layer isn't uneven or too thick, as it will not cook well.

—Instead of using a rolling pin, you can also flatten the ball of dough in your palm and pinch it into a shallow cup. Place 2 tbsp of stuffing in the middle and gently bring together the outer dough while pressing the stuffing in to keep it tight. Join and seal the edges. This method is a bit tricky, so use the one that suits you.

—The traditional and most preferred method of cooking the *litti* is to bake the filled balls over coal or cow dung cakes.

—You can also bake the *littis* in an oven. Place the *littis* on a well-greased baking tray. Preheat the oven to 200 degrees Celsius for 20 minutes, and then bake the *littis* for 10 to 15 minutes. Once done, remove the tray, flip the *littis*, and bake for another 10 minutes.

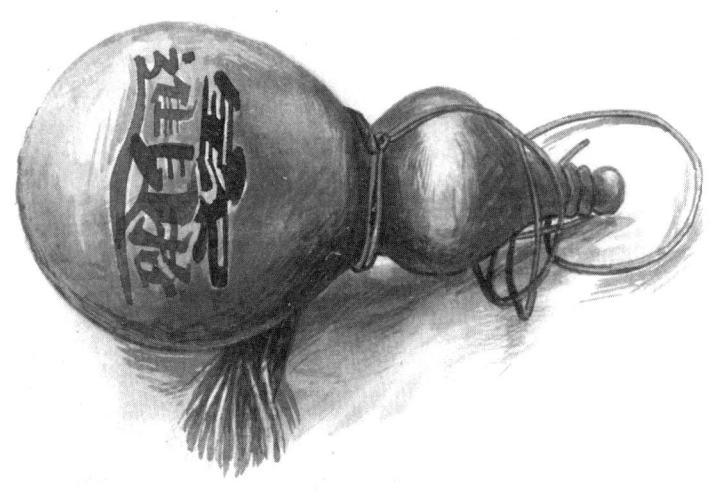

CURRIES AND GRAVIES

Nadan Kozhi Thengapal Curry ✦ Tamarind Chicken ✦ Usha Bhandari's Chicken Saaru ✦ Chicken Afghani ✦ Kashmiri Chicken Curry ✦ Kamala's Chicken Makhani ✦ Varutharacha Meen Curry ✦ Sri Lankan Fish Curry ✦ Tomato Fish Curry ✦ Mithila Fish Curry ✦ Bangdache Hooman ✦ Gwadri Machi Bhatt ✦ Paragon Prawn Mango Curry ✦ Pandi Curry ✦ Sopan Muller's Avial ✦ Vegetable Stew ✦ Butter and Milk Vegetable ✦ Ishwar's Vegetable Kadhi ✦ Kenyan Channa Bateta ✦ Lakshmi Devi's Vegetable Korma ✦ Devi's Vegetable Korma ✦ Mudre Kanni ✦ Lakshmi Devi's Vada Curry ✦ Manga Kutaan ✦ Beetroot Rasam ✦ Sumana's Gokarna Kai Rasa ✦ Sumana's Gokarna Sambrani ✦ Gauri Lankesh's Urgent Saaru ✦ Soppu Cream Saaru ✦ Raw Jackfruit Curry ✦ Baimbale Curry ✦ Pineapple Curry ✦ Pappu ✦ Bele Saaru ✦ Bassaaru ✦ 3-in-1 Bassaaru, Palya, and Chutney ✦ Avarekai Masale Saaru ✦ Molake Hulli

Nadan Kozhi Thengapal Curry

(Chicken Curry with Coconut Milk)

Omana Eappen

Serves 4

750 g country chicken or free-range chicken
1 large onion
2-inch piece of ginger
8 small green chillies
8 cloves of garlic
12–15 curry leaves
2 potatoes
1 tbsp coriander powder
Turmeric powder as required
½ tsp black pepper powder
1 cinnamon stick
2 cloves
½ tsp fennel seeds
¼ cup coconut oil
½ tsp mustard seeds
1 tsp salt
½ tsp malt vinegar
½ coconut
2 cups water

Grate and grind coconut in a mixer-grinder and squeeze out ½ cup of coconut milk through a sieve for the thick first milk. Add 1 cup of water and repeat grinding. Squeeze through sieve for the second milk. Add 1 more cup of water and repeat as above for the third milk. Keep all three separately.

Dice chicken according to the required size. Marinate with turmeric powder and salt (as required) for 1 hour. Then wash the chicken pieces and keep aside. Cut ginger and garlic into small pieces and slit chillies into two. Finely chop onions. Peel and slice potatoes. Powder cinnamon, cloves, and fennel seeds together and keep aside.

Heat coconut oil in a pressure cooker and add mustard seeds. When they pop, add curry leaves, then onion, garlic, ginger, and chillies and stir until they become reddish brown. Mix ½ tsp turmeric powder, coriander powder, pepper, cinnamon, cloves, and fennel seed powder, with a splash of water. Cook till done (i.e. the *masala* should not smell raw). Add chicken pieces and potato slices and stir-fry. Then add the second coconut milk. Add salt and vinegar and mix well. Close the pressure cooker and turn up the flame to high. When it begins to steam, put the weighted pressure regulator on and let it simmer on a low flame for about 15 minutes. Turn off the flame and cool before opening the lid. Depending on the quantity of gravy required, add the third milk and also check for salt. The third milk is optional.

At the time of serving, warm on a low flame, add first milk and immediately switch off, else it will curdle.

Serve hot with rice, *appam,* or *roti.*

Tamarind Chicken

Kadamboor Neeraj

Serves 6–8

1 full chicken (curry cut)

MARINADE:
1 tbsp turmeric powder
1 tsp red chilli powder
2 tsp crushed black peppercorns
1 tsp salt
¼ cup water

CURRY:
A handful of dried tamarind
4 large tomatoes
3 large onions
1 thumb-sized piece of ginger
3 green chillies
1 sprig of curry leaves
1 tsp asafoetida
Salt to taste
1 tsp cumin seeds
1 tsp fenugreek seeds
2 tsp turmeric powder
1 tsp red chilli powder
2 tsp black pepper powder (coarse)
A handful of coriander leaves
2 tbsp oil

Wash the chicken and marinate in all the powders mixed with ¼ cup water. Set aside for at least half an hour. Refrigerate if you're keeping it for longer.

Slit green chillies, finely chop ginger and onions. Make slits in the skin of the tomatoes and boil them. Remove the tomatoes once they are boiled and the skin begins to peel. Use the same water to soak tamarind, squeeze the juice, strain, and set aside. Peel off skin from the tomatoes and mash them.

In a thick-bottomed pot, heat some oil. Throw in cumin seeds and let it splutter. Then add fenugreek seeds, asafoetida, and a few curry leaves. Add green chillies and ginger, and let them blister. Add onions and sauté. Add in mashed tomatoes. Add marinated chicken and sauté. Pour in tamarind water. Add turmeric powder, red chilli powder, black pepper powder, and salt. Add more water if you require more gravy. Cook on a low flame for 25 to 30 minutes until the chicken is tender.

Heat a little oil in a tempering spoon and add curry leaves; once they turn crisp add to the chicken when it is cooked. Garnish with finely-chopped coriander leaves.

Serve with rice or *chapati*.

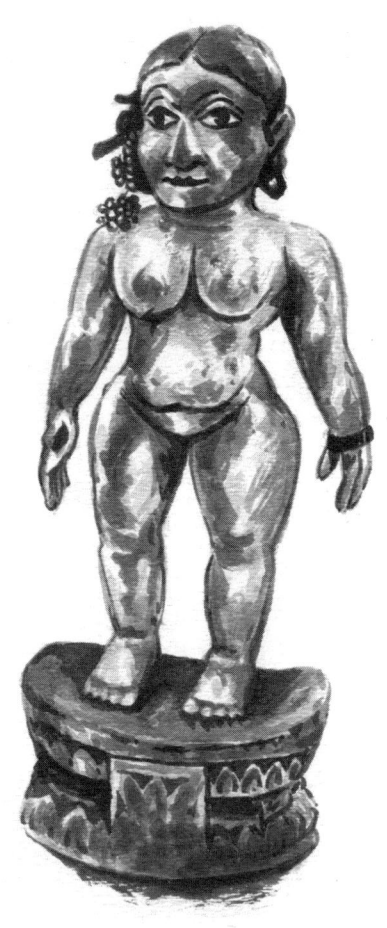

Usha Bhandari's Chicken Saaru

Pushpamala N

Serves 6–8

1 kg chicken (curry cut)
1 onion
6 cloves of garlic
1-inch piece of ginger
A small bunch of coriander leaves
1 lime
2 tbsp oil
Water as required

MARINADE:
1 cup curd
1 tsp salt

MASALA:
¼ coconut
4 green chillies
2 cinnamon sticks
3 cloves
3 pods of green cardamom
1 tsp turmeric powder
1 tsp cumin powder
½ tsp mustard seeds
1 tsp coriander powder
3 red chillies
1 small onion

Marinate chicken with curd and salt. Keep aside for 1 hour. Finely chop onion, garlic, and ginger.

Chop coconut and the small onion. Dry roast all the other ingredients under *masala* and grind them in a mixer-grinder together with chopped coconut and onion.

In a pan, heat oil and add onion, ginger, and garlic. Cook until they turn brown. Add in ground *masala* and fry. Add in chicken pieces and fry for 10 minutes. Add water as required and cook till done. Finally add the juice of 1 lime and garnish with coriander leaves.

Serve with steamed rice or *roti*.

Notes:
—This recipe is originally from Usha Bhandari's contribution to Prajamata Diwali Special 1989 and has been a favourite at home.

Chicken Afghani

Arshi Irshad Ahmadzai

Serves 4

750 g chicken
12 cashew nuts
2 large onions
½ tsp *kasuri methi*
2 tbsp cream
1 tbsp olive oil
50 g butter
Salt to taste

MARINADE:
½ cup curd
1½ tsp ginger-garlic paste
½ tsp crushed black peppercorns
2 pods of green cardamom
½ tsp lime juice

GARNISH:
10–15 coriander or basil leaves

Cut chicken into large pieces, wash, and marinate with curd, ginger-garlic paste, crushed black peppercorns, crushed cardamom, and lime juice for at least 3 hours. Marination time can be longer. Make a paste with cashew nuts and keep aside. Finely chop onions.

Take a deep frying pan, add butter and olive oil. Add marinated chicken pieces into the pan, fry, and remove onto a plate. In the same oil, add finely-chopped onions and fry till they turn light brown. Add cashew nut paste and salt. Sauté this paste for 3 minutes on a medium flame, then add the already fried chicken pieces into the gravy. Cook for 15 minutes on a low flame. Add *kasuri methi* and cream at the end.

Garnish with finely-chopped coriander or basil leaves and serve with *naan-e-khushk* or butter *naan*.

Notes:
—This recipe is from my grandfather Anaytullah Khan who tried to amalgamate Indian and Afghani cuisines.

Kashmiri Chicken Curry

Dr. Lakshmi Devi

Serves 4

500 g chicken
½ cup *ghee*
1 big onion
5 pods of green cardamom
2 tomatoes
1½ tsp red chilli powder
1½ cup buttermilk
¼ cup almond paste
Salt to taste
Water as required

GINGER-GARLIC PASTE:
4 cloves of garlic
4 small pieces of ginger
½ cup water

GARNISH:
½ cup cream
¼ cup cashew nuts

Chop ginger and garlic and grind into a paste with ½ a cup of water. Chop onion and tomatoes into medium-sized pieces. Cut chicken into curry-sized pieces. Roast cashew nuts. Keep aside.

Heat *ghee* in a thick-bottomed pan, till it begins to smoke, and drop in cardamom and chopped onions. Stir till it becomes light brown and add ginger-garlic paste. Stir briskly for 5 minutes. Now add chicken pieces, cut tomatoes, and red chilli powder. Stir again for 5 minutes. Next, add buttermilk, almond paste, water as required, and salt to taste. Cook on low flame till the chicken is done. Remove from flame and top it with cream and roasted cashew nuts.

Serve hot with rice or *pulao*.

Kamala's Chicken Makhani

Sapna Chandu

Serves 4

4 chicken breasts
2 tbsp cooking oil
1 big white onion
2 cloves of garlic
1½ cinnamon sticks
2–3 tsp salt
210 g concentrated tomato paste
2 tbsp premium quality curry powder
1 cup coriander leaves
150 ml cooking cream

Dice chicken into small 1-cm pieces (holds the flavor more than large pieces). Dice onion and garlic.

In a small pot, mix tomato paste, curry powder, and chopped coriander leaves and heat until it bubbles. Add a little water, so it mixes well, and keep aside.

In a large pot heat oil, add cinnamon, and fry for a minute so it flavours the oil and fills the air with its tantalizing aroma. Add diced onion and garlic, and fry on medium heat until onion cooks lightly.

Add chicken and fry till browned. Add 2 to 3 tsp salt (or to taste) and mix well. Now take the tomato sauce prepared earlier and stir in well. Simmer on low for 5 minutes (or until chicken is cooked but still tender). Finally add cream, mix well, and cook for 1 to 2 minutes.

Serve with brown/white *basmati* rice, *chapati*, and yoghurt or *raita*.

Notes:
—The curry powder you use can be mild or hot—Bolst's Curry Powder for example.

—This light and uniquely delicious version of the popularly known butter chicken is an adaptation by my Mum (Kamala) and has taken Melbourne by storm. An invitation to come home for Kamala's chicken *makhani* is widely sought after in my circle of family and friends, and her recipe has circulated far and wide in our Melbourne community.

—Though quick and simple to prepare, this dish is a fine balance of spice and fragrance and is susceptible to being overwhelmed by one or the other.

Some tips to find your balance:
—Add half a small green chilli for extra spice or use hot curry powder. Do be careful if adjusting the amount of curry powder—too much can be too heavy on the palate.

—You can also vary the amount of coriander leaves according to taste though its presence should be felt but not heard.

—Too much cinnamon can be overbearing. Less is more.

—Finally, you can add more or less cream depending on desired level of spiciness and depth of flavour. Enjoy!

Varutharacha Meen Curry

(Fish Curry with Fried and Crushed Masala)

Shivaji Panikkar

Serves 8–9

1 kg cleaned fish
8–10 shallots
2 green chillies
A handful of curry leaves
4-inch piece of ginger
15–18 cloves of garlic
3 tbsp coriander powder
3 tbsp Kashmiri or Deggi chilli powder
2 tbsp turmeric powder
6–7 black peppercorns
4–5 pieces of *kudampuli*
1½ cups water
Coconut oil as required
Salt to taste

Cut fish into medium-sized pieces. Finely chop shallots, garlic, and ginger.

Add some coconut oil to a pan and fry shallots, garlic, and ginger. Add curry leaves and slit green chillies, followed by coriander powder, turmeric powder, chilli powder, and crushed peppercorns. Fry for about 30 seconds. Add *kudampuli* and salt. Pour 1½ cups of water and once it boils, add fish and cook with the lid closed on a low flame for 15 to 20 minutes. Before turning off the flame, add more curry leaves and coconut oil, and gently rotate the pan to spread the oil well.

Serve with rice and coconut chutney. This curry tastes better a day after it is cooked as the fish absorbs the *masalas* better overnight.

Notes:
—Sardine, mackerel, tuna, pomfret, pearl spot, or king fish can be used.

—*Kudampuli* is a sour fruit, a variety of kokum, available in South-Western Coastal India.

Sri Lankan Fish Curry

Thisath Thoradeniya

Serves 4–6

500 g tuna
1 kg tomatoes
200 g onions
2–3 green chillies
1 cup water
½ tsp red chilli powder
A handful of curry leaves
¼ tsp turmeric powder
1 tsp mustard seeds
1 tsp crushed black peppercorns
A few cloves
A few crushed pods of green cardamom
1 cinnamon stick
Coconut oil (or any other cooking oil) as required
Salt to taste
2 tbsp crushed ginger and garlic

SRI LANKAN CURRY POWDER:
1 tsp coriander seeds
1 tsp cumin seeds
1 tsp fennel seeds

If you are using fresh fish, cut into chunks, wash, and leave aside. If you are using canned fish, then open the lid and drain out the brine.

Cut onions and tomatoes into chunks; slit green chillies. Grind coriander seeds, cumin seeds, and fennel seeds together to make Sri Lankan curry powder.

Heat oil in a pan. Throw in mustard seeds. Once they crackle, add green chillies, onions, tomatoes, and curry leaves. Stir for a while and add water to form enough gravy. Add turmeric powder, red chilli powder, Sri Lankan curry powder, crushed peppercorns, ginger, garlic, cloves, cardamom, and cinnamon. Add salt to taste. Add fish and cook for 10 to 15 minutes on a medium flame.

Serve with *roti, paratha*, bread, or rice.

Notes:
—The tuna can be canned or fresh, or any other chunky fish can be used. This is a curry that takes less time to cook but feeds many.

—Prawns could be added into the same sauce instead of fish. It is best to fry the prawns a bit before adding it into the gravy.

Tomato Fish Curry

Dr. Lakshmi Devi

Serves 4–6

1 kg fish
Oil for frying

MARINADE:
1 tsp red chilli powder
¼ tsp turmeric powder
Salt to taste

GRAVY:
2–3 green chillies
4 cloves of garlic
2-inch piece of ginger
500 g tomatoes
2 onions
4 tsp oil
1 tsp red chilli powder
¼ tsp turmeric powder
A few sprigs of coriander leaves
Salt to taste

Clean and cut fish into curry-sized pieces. Marinate with chilli powder, turmeric powder, and salt and set aside for an hour. Shallow-fry till cooked and remove.

Grind green chillies, garlic, and ginger into a paste. Finely chop onions and tomatoes. In a pan, heat 4 tsp of oil and add onions and tomatoes with ginger-garlic-chilli paste. Add in chilli powder, turmeric powder, and salt, and cook till the gravy is done. Add fried fish to the gravy, let it simmer for a few minutes, and garnish with coriander leaves.

Serve with hot rice.

Mithila Fish Curry

Muskaan Singh & Murari Jha

Serves 5–6

2 kg *rohu*
2 tbsp salt
1 cup curd
1 sprig of coriander leaves
250 g mustard oil for frying

MARINADE:
1 tbsp garlic paste
2 tbsp red chilli powder
2 tbsp turmeric powder
1 tbsp salt

GRAVY:
500 g onions
2 tomatoes
4 tbsp mustard seeds
2 bay leaves
2 dry red chillies
2 tbsp garlic paste
1 tbsp red chilli powder
2 tbsp turmeric powder
1 tbsp salt
2 tbsp coriander powder

Wash fish thoroughly with curd and salt to remove the smell and then cut into chunks. Marinate with garlic paste, red chilli powder, turmeric powder, and salt for 15 minutes.

Make a paste of onions in a mixer-grinder and finely chop tomatoes. Make a paste of mustard seeds and set aside.

Heat mustard oil in the *kadhai*, shallow-fry fish, remove, and keep aside. In the remaining oil, add bay leaves, dry red chillies, onion paste, garlic paste, red chilli powder, turmeric powder, salt, tomatoes, coriander powder, and fry for 15 minutes till the gravy is cooked. Add mustard paste to the *kadhai* and fry for 10 minutes. Add water according to the thickness of gravy you prefer. Once the water comes to a boil, put in the fried fish, and cook for 20 minutes.

Garnish with coriander leaves and serve with plain rice and salad.

Notes:

—Traditionally the fish used is *rohu*, but it can be substituted with *catla* or tilapia.

—Fish curry from Mithila in Bihar has its own cultural and historical value. It is a prestigious dish offered to guests. The head of the fish is offered to show respect, a tail piece to show contempt.

—The flag of the erstwhile princely state of Darbhanga had a fish as its insignia. The fish motif is central to Mithila's traditional folk art form, and is considered an auspicious symbol.

—A newly wed daughter-in-law is judged based on her fish curry.

—Along with fish curry, fried fish, egg *pakora,* and fish pickles are traditional delicacies of the region.

Bangdache Hooman

(Mackerel Curry)

Shyamli Singbal

Serves 4

3 mackerels (*bangda*)
2 cups water

MARINADE:
½ tsp turmeric powder
½ tsp salt

CURRY PASTE:
½ coconut
A marble-sized ball of tamarind
4 Cancona dry red chillies
½ tsp turmeric powder
½-inch piece of ginger

SEASONING:
½-inch piece of ginger
6–8 fresh Sichuan peppercorns
3–4 dry kokum
Salt to taste
1 green chilli

Chop mackerels into 2-inch pieces and marinate with turmeric powder and salt for 20 minutes.

For the curry paste, grate coconut and cut the ½-inch piece of ginger. In a mixer-grinder, grind these to a fine paste with the other ingredients listed under curry paste, adding water as required. Transfer to a bowl and set aside.

In a saucepan, add the curry paste and 2 cups of water. Bruise and add Sichuan peppercorns. Julienne the other piece of ginger and add, with salt to taste. Bring to a boil, stirring occasionally.

Once it is boiling, lower the flame and let the curry simmer for 2 minutes. Now add the marinated fish pieces and dried kokum. Cook for 3 to 4 minutes. Once the fish has cooked, add slit green chilli just before taking the curry off the flame.

Serve with *ukhde tandool* (Goan brown rice) or plain white steamed rice.

Notes:
—If it is too spicy, add some freshly grated coconut on top.

—Statements made by my mom I would happily second: "When I want to eat bangda curry, I will eat it" and "Every day is an occasion to eat fish curry and rice!"

Gwadri Machi Bhatt

(Gwadri Fish and Rice)

Sohail Abdullah

Serves 6

BHATT:
500 g *basmati* rice
500 g potatoes
⅔ cup vegetable oil
10 sprigs of curry leaves
1 cup garlic-coriander-green-chilli paste
⅔ cup dill leaves, loosely packed
2 tbsp coriander seeds
2 tbsp cumin seeds
1 tsp turmeric powder
2 tsp red chilli powder
2 tbsp salt
5 cups water

MACHI:
500 g fish
¼ cup vegetable oil
5 sprigs of curry leaves
⅓ cup dill leaves, loosely packed
½ cup garlic-coriander-chilli paste
2 tsp coriander seeds
2 tsp cumin seeds
½ tsp turmeric powder
2 tsp red chilli powder
1 tsp salt (or according to taste)
1 cup water

For the *bhatt*, wash and soak rice for 30 minutes; peel and quarter potatoes. Heat oil on a medium flame in a heavy-bottomed lidded pot. Add potatoes and fry for a few minutes. To this add curry leaves, dill leaves, and coriander-chilli-garlic paste. Fry for a few minutes, on medium flame, then add crushed cumin seeds, crushed coriander seeds, turmeric powder, red chilli powder, and salt. Fry for 2 more minutes and mix in rice along with 5 cups of water. Cover and bring to a boil. Then, reduce heat and cook till the rice absorbs the water. Stir the rice again and cook on very low heat for about 15 minutes.

For the *machi,* heat oil in a pot on medium heat. Add curry leaves, dill leaves, and garlic-coriander-chilli paste. Fry for 2 minutes and add crushed coriander seeds, crushed cumin seeds, turmeric powder, red chilli powder, and salt and stir.

Add fish; fry for 2 to 3 minutes and add a cup of water. Cook uncovered on a medium-low flame for about 15 minutes (or till done) and remove from fire.

Serve both together with yogurt and sliced onions on the side. The rice by itself without the fish curry is also delicious and makes a great meal of leftovers the next day.

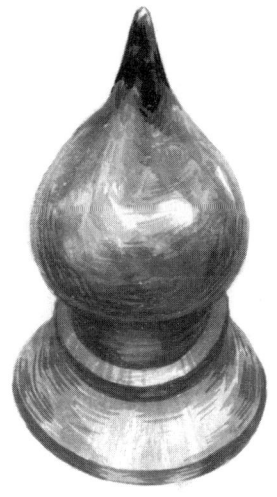

Notes:
—We tend to make this with a kind of mackerel but it works with any kind of fish that's firm enough to not entirely fall apart while being cooked.

—For the garlic-coriander-chilli paste, blend together 3 handfuls of coriander leaves with stems, 5 or 6 medium-sized (medium heat) green chillies, and peeled garlic cloves from 3 medium-sized bulbs, in ¼ cup of water.

—My sister and I wrote this recipe down from observing our mother Zubeda Malik who cooks with all her heart and measures nothing. This is our Gwadri-Kutchi-Ismaili family's version of the recipe.

—In Gwadar, and in Gwadri households in Karachi, this would be made on the first day of the lunar months and weddings, specifically for lunch on the day of the *mehndi*. Now it's also our go-to Sunday family lunch.

Paragon Prawn Mango Curry

Nihaal Faizal

Serves 4

250 g prawns
1 raw mango
1 onion
1-inch piece of ginger
3 cloves of garlic
2 tomatoes
4 green chillies
5 tsp coconut oil
¼ tsp fenugreek seeds
2 tsp Kashmiri chilli powder
1 tsp turmeric powder
1 tsp tamarind pulp
Salt to taste
1 cup water
½ cup thick coconut milk

GARNISH:
A few curry leaves

Finely chop onion, ginger, garlic, and tomatoes. Slit green chillies. Peel the skin off raw mango and use a peeler to grate its flesh into flat, long pieces.

Heat oil in a *kadhai*. Once hot, add fenugreek seeds. Sauté and add onion, green chillies, ginger, and garlic. Sauté and let it cook. When it turns golden-brown, add tomato and cook till the raw smell is gone. Add chilli powder, turmeric powder, tamarind pulp, and salt to taste. Cook for a few minutes, add water and prawns. Cook for a few minutes till the prawns are half-done. Add grated mango and cook until the prawns are fully done. Finally, lower the flame, add coconut milk, cook for 1 minute, and turn off the flame.

Garnish with curry leaves and serve hot with rice.

Notes:
—Instead of grating, the raw mango can also be sliced, but grating is preferred as it lends a richer flavour.

—The recipe can be made spicier, if preferred, by adding more chillies.

—This recipe, from Paragon restaurant in Calicut, was published in *Vanitha* magazine. It was originally a recipe for a fish curry (seer fish preferred) but my mother, Zarine Faizal, developed this variation with prawns instead.

—This is a recipe that is a staple at all Reliable Copy dinners and by extension, gets taken to potlucks at 1Shanthiroad as well.

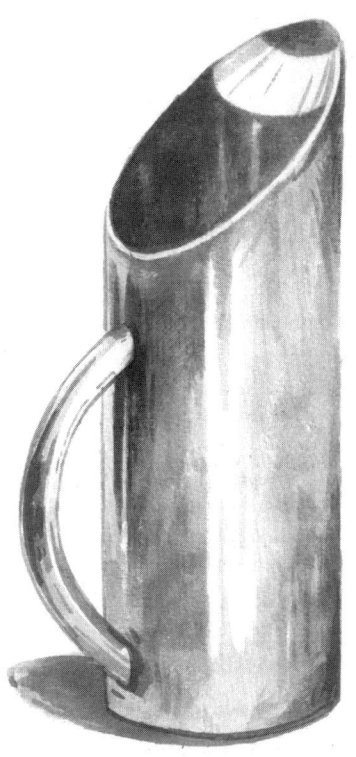

Pandi Curry

(Pork Curry)

Smitha Cariappa

Serves 6–8

1 kg pork (including fatty pieces)
1 tsp turmeric powder
1 tsp red chilli powder
Salt to taste
2 tsp *kachampuli*
3 cups water

MASALA:
1 tsp black peppercorns
5 cinnamon sticks
6 cloves
1 tsp cumin seeds
2 tsp coriander

PASTE:
1 cup chopped onions
1-inch piece of ginger
5 cloves of garlic
5 green chillies
1 tsp cumin seeds

Cut pork into curry-sized pieces and marinate with turmeric powder, chilli powder, and salt. Set aside for 15 minutes.

Heat a pan on low flame and dry roast ingredients for the *masala*, making sure nothing burns. Grind into a powder and keep aside. Grind ginger, garlic, onions, green chillies, and cumin seeds into a fine paste. Add to the marinated pork and mix well. Boil 3 cups of water and add in pork, as well as the ground *masala*. Stir well, cover, and cook until pork is tender and gravy is thick. Add in *kachampuli*, stir, and remove immediately from the heat.

Serve hot with steamed rice.

Notes:
—*Kachampuli* is a dark, tart vinegar used in Coorgi dishes and is available in Bangalore near Kodava Samaj or the Ham and Pork Shop.

Sopan Muller's Avial

Sandeep TK

Serves 6–8

100 g white pumpkin
2 brinjals
1 small snake gourd
100 g ivy gourd
2 drumsticks
1 Madras cucumber
½ tsp turmeric powder
Salt to taste
4 cups water
1 cup curd

PASTE:
1 coconut
15 curry leaves
1 tbsp cumin seeds
A couple of green chillies

TEMPERING:
4 tbsp coconut oil
1 tbsp cumin seeds
10 curry leaves

Peel and cut pumpkin, brinjal, snake gourd, ivy gourd, drumsticks, and Madras cucumber into fairly large pieces or cubes. Grate coconut and blend in a mixer-grinder with curry leaves, 1 tbsp of cumin seeds, and slit green chillies to form a coarse paste.

In a large pot, add 4 cups of water, turmeric powder, and salt. Add cut vegetables and cook on an open flame until they are soft. Drain the water and retain it. Add ground coconut paste to the vegetables and cook for a few minutes on a medium flame, till the coconut *masala* is also cooked. Add 1 cup of the drained water back into the pot. Finally, add curd, simmer for another 2 to 3 minutes, adjust salt, and turn off.

In a tempering spoon, heat coconut oil and add 1 tbsp of cumin seeds. When they start spluttering and turn brown, add curry leaves. Add this tempering to the vegetables in the pot.

Serve with hot rice.

Vegetable Stew

Sarasija Subramanian

Serves 4–6

150 g French beans
150 g broad beans
150 g carrots
100 g potatoes
2 large onions
100 g green peas
5 tbsp coconut oil
400 ml thick coconut milk
500 ml milk
1 tsp sugar
1 tsp salt

TEMPERING:
2 sprigs of curry leaves
5 small green chillies
8–10 cloves
1 cinnamon stick
1 tbsp crushed black peppercorns
2 tbsp coconut oil

Chop French beans, broad beans, carrots, and potatoes into thin pieces—1 to 1½ inches long. Slit green chillies down the middle, cut onions into square chunks, and shell peas.

Heat 5 tbsp of coconut oil in a thick-bottomed deep pan or a large pressure cooker. Add 10 to 15 curry leaves, 3 green chillies, 5 cloves, and a cinnamon stick. Wait for them to simmer for a minute and then add ½ tbsp of crushed peppercorns and 2 chopped onions. Add 1 tsp salt and 1 tsp sugar. The sugar will caramelize the onions slightly. Once the onions turn reddish-brown, add chopped potatoes. Close the pan and allow potatoes to cook, stirring it every few minutes to make sure it doesn't stick.

Wait for the potatoes to half-cook and add chopped French and broad beans. Keep closed for 5 to 7 minutes, then add carrots. Add salt to taste and stir the vegetables for 5 to 7 minutes more. Add a few more spoons of coconut oil, if required. Once done, pour in coconut milk from the Tetra Pak, along with 500 ml of milk. Let the milk boil and then add green peas. Within a minute, turn off the gas, cover, and keep aside.

Before serving, heat 2 tbsp of coconut oil in a tempering spoon. Add 8 to 10 curry leaves, the remaining 2 green chillies, the leftover crushed peppercorns, and cloves. Allow them to simmer for a few minutes, then add into the stew. Close the lid, so the smell stays trapped.

Serve hot with rice, *dosa,* or *appam.*

Notes:
—Keep all the vegetables chopped and in different bowls; they must be added into the pan in order of how long they take to cook.

—I usually use the store-bought coconut milk Tetra Pak. If preparing coconut milk at home: grate a fresh coconut and grind the flesh with 1 glass of water. Transfer the ground coconut into a soft muslin cloth or fine sieve and squeeze out the milk. Keep this first batch of milk separate. Repeat this grinding and squeezing twice more and keep the second and third batch of milk in another vessel. If you are using this, add the thin second and third batch of coconut milk a few minutes after you add the carrots. After the milk has boiled and the gas is turned off, add the first batch of thick milk and mix it in.

—If you need to store the dish and reheat it the next day, add a little water while re-heating and ½ a cup of coconut milk once it is heated. You can also repeat the last serving step of tempering for extra flavour.

Butter and Milk Vegetable

Arshad Hakim

Serves 8–10

150 g yam
2 potatoes
200 g French beans
100 g broccoli
100 g baby corn
100 g mushroom
2 carrots
2 capsicums
2–3 tbsp oil
100 g table butter
5–6 cloves of garlic
A handful of curry leaves
1 l milk
1 tsp sugar
Salt to taste

Chop yam, potato, baby corn, carrots, and capsicum into strips; green beans into long pieces—approximately an inch long. Chop mushrooms in half and separate broccoli into florets. Sauté all the vegetables in a pan with 2 to 3 tbsp of oil till they are fully cooked. Do not add water, as they should retain their crunchiness. Add them in the pan according to the speed in which they cook—follow the order in the ingredients list.

In a thick-bottomed pot, melt butter and add garlic (either chopped or crushed) and curry leaves. Let it cook until the garlic becomes brown. Then add milk, sugar, and salt to this pot and let it boil until the milk reduces and becomes crumbly. Once done, transfer this into the pan with the sautéed vegetables and mix. Check for seasoning.

Serve hot with pasta *aglio e olio*, bread, or rice.

Notes:
—The point is to use vegetables that aren't juicy so that once they are cooked they become crunchy.

—This dish can also be made with meat or chicken.

Ishwar's Vegetable Kadhi

Aaiushi Beniwal

Serves 3–4

2 onions
4 tomatoes
1 potato
100 g cluster beans
100 g ivy gourd
5–6 Cubanelle peppers (*bajji mirch*)
10 black peppercorns
1 tsp mustard seeds
1 tsp cumin seeds
2 tbsp oil

BASE:
400 ml buttermilk
4 heaped tbsp gram flour
Water as required
1 cup sour curd
2-inch piece of ginger
4–5 green chillies
½ tbsp turmeric powder
Salt to taste

TEMPERING:
3 tbsp *ghee*
8 cloves of garlic
4 sprigs of curry leaves
100 g spring onions

GARNISH:
3 tbsp coriander leaves
1 lime

Cut onions and Cubanelle peppers into medium-sized chunks, slice tomatoes, potato, and ivy gourd lengthwise, and chop cluster beans into 1-inch pieces. Chop shoots of spring onion into 2-inch pieces and finely dice the bulb. Crush peppercorns, slit green chillies, smash ginger, and finely chop garlic.

To prepare the base, mix gram flour and ½ a cup of water into a smooth paste. In a large bowl, pour in buttermilk and slowly mix in the gram flour paste, passing it through a sieve to make sure there are no lumps. Once mixed, add sour curd and mix well. Add in an equal amount of water (water to base ratio should be 1:1).

Next, add ginger and green chillies, a few pinches of turmeric powder, and salt to season the base. Cook this on a low flame in a thick-bottomed pot. Keep stirring every now and then to make sure the gram flour doesn't stick to the bottom. Cook until it begins to bubble and rise. Once this mixture has risen 3 to 4 times, take it off the heat.

While the base is cooking on a low flame, heat oil in another deep pan. Add peppercorns and mustard seeds, wait till they pop, and then add cumin seeds. Add chopped potato, onions, and spring onion bulbs. Once these are half-cooked, add cluster beans and ivy gourd. Also add a pinch of turmeric powder and salt to taste. Once the beans and ivy gourd are half-cooked, add Cubanelle peppers, fry for a few minutes, and add the gram flour and buttermilk mix. Lastly, add tomatoes and bring to a boil (the tomatoes only need to be steamed, so add them only once the stew starts to simmer). After it starts to bubble, boil for about 15 minutes (or till all the vegetables have cooked). Once done, turn off the heat.

To temper, heat *ghee* in a tempering pan, add chopped garlic, chopped spring onions greens, and curry leaves. Once the garlic is brown and the leaves are crispy (the leaves only need a flash in the pan to get crisp), add them to the *kadhi*.

Garnish with finely-chopped coriander leaves and the juice of a lime. Serve hot with plain *ghee* rice, *parathas,* or *khichdi*.

Notes:
—The buttermilk used in this dish should preferably be sour.

—The gram flour has a tendency to become lumpy, so do not add the gram flour directly into the buttermilk.

—Use small spicy green chillies.

—If the *kadhi* is too spicy or too thick, add more plain buttermilk; to cut the spice, and/or increase sourness, add a bit more lime juice.

—If it is too sour, add plain, unfermented buttermilk. Adjust heat and sourness according to taste.

—The origin of this style of making *kadhi* lies in the hands of my father. This is a take on the North-Indian *kadhi*, which is a staple, and is usually prepared without vegetables. My dad was quite the genius in the kitchen when it came to adding a twist to regular dishes and creating healthier versions of North-Indian staples. My version is more sour compared to his. Taking his lead, I keep trying different vegetables with it. It is a versatile dish—don't hesitate to try different combinations!

Variations:
As the dish is versatile, you can pick and choose which vegetables to add. You can also experiment and add vegetables which are not mentioned, but here are some combinations that have worked for me:

—Beans like *tuvar* (green *toor*), cluster beans, ivy gourd, and peas—a handful of each.

—Dill leaves, *tuvar*, and onions. This is a Gujarati combination made during winter, when these two vegetables are in season. The method remains the same.

—Greens like spinach, amaranthus, or fenugreek leaves. Be careful of the ratios between the leafy greens and the base. Don't overdo the leaves, as they will overpower the palate.

—The coriander leaves in the garnish can be replaced with only chopped spring onions or mint leaves, which will alter the flavour of the dish to a great extent.

Kenyan Channa Bateta

(Kenyan Chickpea Potato Stew)

Ragini Bhow

Serves 4

1 kg baby potatoes
3 green chillies
½ raw mango
850 g canned chickpeas (2 cans)
1 can full-fat coconut milk
3 cups water
1 lime
1 tbsp grated ginger
2 ½ tsp turmeric powder
1 ½ tsp salt
1 tsp sugar
10–15 curry leaves
2 tbsp oil

GARNISH:
1 sprig of coriander leaves
1 tsp red chilli powder
4 lime wedges
1 diced red onion
1 tsp cumin powder

Boil baby potatoes, chop green chillies, peel and grate raw mango, and juice a lime.

Heat oil in a pot and add curry leaves, grated mango, salt, sugar, green chillies, grated ginger, turmeric powder, coconut milk, and 3 cups of water. Bring to a boil. After 3 to 5 minutes, add chickpeas, potatoes, and lime juice. Simmer for 20 to 25 minutes with the lid on, stirring every now and then. When the stew feels well-infused and potatoes and chickpeas are cooked through, it is ready.

Serve in individual bowls and garnish with coriander leaves, chilli powder, lime wedges, diced red onions, and cumin powder, with an accompaniment of green chutney and any dry snack—like *'chevdo'*.

Notes:
—You can add mango pickle as garnish for extra spice and tang.

—The canned chickpeas can be replaced with 250 g of raw chickpeas, soaked overnight and pressure cooked for three to four whistles, till well done.

—I've been increasingly interested in learning and sharing recipes that have originated from Indian-African cultural overlaps and celebrating these rare moments. This is a recipe that was shared with me by my Gujarati aunt who has explored plant-based Gujarati cuisine in Kenya and Tanzania.

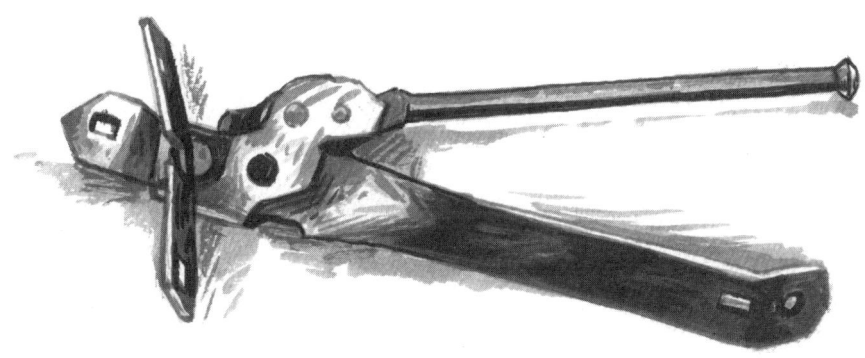

Lakshmi Devi's Vegetable Korma

Dr. Hemalatha Bhuvanendra

Serves 8

250 g green peas
250 g broad beans
2 carrots
100 g beans
2 potatoes
1 capsicum
1 tbsp salt
1 glass water
2 tbsp oil

MASALA:
1 tbsp oil
5–7 cloves of garlic
1 thumb-sized piece of ginger
4 green chillies
2 onions
1 tomato
4 cloves
2 small cinnamon sticks
A handful of coriander leaves
A handful of grated coconut
1 tsp coriander powder
A pinch of turmeric powder

Chop broad beans, carrots, beans, potatoes, capsicum, tomato, and onions. Finely chop garlic, ginger, and green chillies.

Heat 1 tbsp of oil in a *kadhai* and add chopped garlic, ginger, and green chillies and fry till golden-brown. Add onions and fry until they become pink. Then add tomatoes, cloves, cinnamon, and coriander leaves and fry for 2 minutes. Remove from heat and cool for 5 to 10 minutes. Blend these ingredients in a mixer-grinder with grated coconut, turmeric powder, and coriander powder. Keep aside.

Heat 2 tbsp of oil in a *kadhai* and add in all the chopped vegetables along with peas. Fry for 5 to 7 minutes till they become slightly soft. Add in the ground *masala* with about 1 tbsp salt and a big glass of water. Boil for about 15 minutes.

Serve with *ragi mudde*, rice, *poori,* or *chapati*.

Devi's Vegetable Korma

Devi Raju

Serves 15

250 g beans
250 g carrots
4 potatoes
250 g cauliflower
250 g broad beans
2 kohlrabis
2 capsicums
1 tsp coriander powder
½ tsp *garam masala*
1 l water
2 tbsp salt
2 cups curd

MASALA:
2 coconuts
10 green chillies
10 cloves
2 cinnamon sticks
1 pod of green cardamom
2 onions

TEMPERING:
50 g oil
1 cinnamon stick
2 pods of green cardamom
2 bay leaves
2 tbsp ginger-garlic paste

Break coconut, remove flesh, and blend into a paste in a mixer-grinder with green chillies, cinnamon, cardamom, and cloves. Chop 2 onions and grind them into a paste separately. Mix both the pastes.

Chop beans, carrots, potatoes, cauliflower, broad beans, kohlrabi, and capsicums. Heat oil in a pressure cooker and add cinnamon, green cardamom, bay leaves, and ginger-garlic paste. After a minute, add beans, carrots, potatoescauliflower, broad beans, and kohlrabi. Mix well and add coriander powder and *garam masala*.

Once the vegetables are sautéed, add the mixed paste. Add a litre of water, 2 tbsp salt, and chopped capsicum. Close the pressure cooker, cook for one whistle, and switch off. Once the steam is released, add 2 cups of curd and mix well.

Serve with *chapati* or *roti*.

Notes:
—Capsicum is generally added last because it has a very strong flavour.

—Curd is added after switching off the flame so that it doesn't curdle.

Mudre Kanni

(Horse Gram Gravy)

Smitha Cariappa

Serves 10–12

1 kg horse gram
1 l water
1 onion
10 cloves of garlic
A lime-sized ball of tamarind
2-inch piece of jaggery
1 tsp coriander powder
½ tsp turmeric powder
½ tsp red chilli powder
Salt to taste
2 tbsp oil
½ tsp mustard seeds

MASALA:
2 tsp oil
1 tbsp black peppercorns
½ tsp fenugreek seeds
4 dry red chillies
2 tsp cumin seeds

Soak horse gram in water overnight. Chop and grind onion and garlic to a fine paste.

Wash soaked horse gram and pressure cook for 45 minutes in 1 litre water. Strain and preserve the water. Grind 1 cup of cooked horse gram into a fine paste and keep aside. Soak tamarind and jaggery in 1 cup of strained horse gram water. Squeeze and strain. Mix coriander powder, turmeric powder, chilli powder, and salt into the remaining horse gram water.

Heat a pan and add 2 tsp of oil. Add peppercorns, fenugreek seeds, dry chillies, and cumin seeds, one at a time, in the order given, stirring constantly to prevent burning. Allow each ingredient to fry for a few seconds before adding the next, till they are all roasted. Remove from the pan, let them cool, and grind into a fine powder. Mix the powder with the onion and garlic paste.

Heat 2 tbsp of oil in a pan, add mustard seeds, and allow them to splutter. Add the ground *masala* and fry on low heat for 2 minutes, stirring constantly to prevent the *masala* from sticking or burning. Add horse gram water and the tamarind-jaggery water. Mix and cook till gravy is reduced, stirring frequently to avoid burning. To help thicken the gravy, mix in the ground horse gram into the water. When ready it should have the consistency of thin custard.

Serve with boiled rice, *akki rotti*, or steamed *kadambuttu* (rice balls).

Notes:
—The rest of the cooked horse gram can be used for any other purpose, such as another curry.

—*Mudre kanni* can be preserved for several days.

—To help thicken the gravy, a mixture of 1 tbsp rice flour and 2 tbsp water can be used instead of the ground horse gram paste.

Lakshmi Devi's Vada Curry

Suresh Jayaram

Serves 3

4 tbsp gram flour
3 cups water
3 tbsp oil
1 tsp mustard seeds
3 tsp cumin seeds
A handful of curry leaves
1 tsp asafoetida
4 slit green chillies
2 onions
8–10 cloves of garlic
2 tsp ginger-garlic paste
4 tomatoes
A pinch of turmeric powder
½ tsp red chilli powder
1 tsp salt
5–7 *dal vadas*

Mix gram flour in a bowl with 2 cups of water, till it becomes a paste. Make sure there are no lumps. Finely chop onions, garlic, and tomatoes. Heat 2 tbsp oil in a thick-bottomed pot, add mustard seeds, cumin seeds, curry leaves, asafoetida, and slit green chillies and fry. Pour the paste into the pan and add 1 cup of water.

In a separate pan, fry onions and garlic in the remaining oil and add ginger-garlic paste. When half-done, add tomatoes, turmeric powder, chilli powder, and salt. When the onions have turned brown, pour this mixture into the pot with the paste. Once this mixture comes to a boil, add the *vadas*. Cook on high flame for an additional 5 minutes.

Serve hot, with rice.

Notes:
—A great dish if one has leftover *vadas*.

—It's always better to put less salt initially and then add according to taste later. A good way to see if the salt is right is to get a person with a critical tongue to taste and assign them to be the taster of the household!

Manga Kutaan

(Raw Mango Kutaan)

Sarasija Subramanian

Serves 4

2 tbsp sesame oil
2 raw mangoes
500 g white pumpkin
1 tsp turmeric powder
Salt to taste
3 cups water

MASALA:
4 tbsp raw rice
1 cup grated coconut
2 dry red chillies

TEMPERING:
2 tbsp fenugreek seeds
2 dry red chillies
1 tbsp mustard seeds
10–15 curry leaves
2 tbsp sesame oil

Cut raw mango into ½-inch chunks and white pumpkin into 1-inch cubes. Soak 4 tbsp of raw rice in a cup of water for about half an hour. Dry roast 2 whole red chillies till they are slightly brown. Keep aside.

In a deep frying pan, heat 2 tbsp of sesame oil and add mango and pumpkin. Stir them for a few minutes till they slightly change colour. Add turmeric powder and salt to taste. Once they are slightly brown, pour in 3 cups of water (enough to submerge all the vegetables). Bring water to a boil and let the pumpkin and raw mango cook in it.

As this cooks, grind together grated coconut, soaked raw rice, and dry roasted red chillies, with a little bit of water, into a coarse paste. Once the pumpkin and raw mango are cooked (pumpkin should be translucent and soft), add the ground paste and bring it to a boil again. Boil for a few minutes and turn off the gas.

Before serving, heat 2 tbsp of sesame oil in a small pan. Add in 2 red chillies broken in half, fenugreek seeds, mustard seeds, and curry leaves. Let them simmer till the mustard seeds begin to pop, and then pour into the dish, closing the lid immediately to trap the smell in.

Serve with rice and *papad* or chips.

Notes:

—Though it is ideal for you to check the sourness of the raw mango before adding it in, in case it is too sour then you can add a tsp of jaggery into the boiling water while the vegetables cook to balance the flavour.

—Depending on the season, another version of the same dish is a *mambazham kootan,* made with ripe (but firm) mangoes instead of raw mango. Every step remains the same, except that the 2 raw mangoes in the recipe above are replaced with 1 ripe mango. This dish is sweet and spicy, as opposed to sour.

—This dish is very specific to a Palakkad Tamil *brahmin* household, with a signature Kerala twist on an otherwise Tamilian style of cooking.

Beetroot Rasam

Devi Raju

Serves 6

1 beetroot
3 glasses water
A lime-sized ball of tamarind
1 tbsp black peppercorns
½ tbsp cumin seeds
1 onion
2 tomatoes
4–5 cloves of garlic
¼ tbsp turmeric powder
½ tbsp red chilli powder
1 tbsp coriander powder
Salt to taste

TEMPERING:
1 tbsp *ghee*
1 tsp mustard seeds
1 sprig of curry leaves
3 dry red chillies
A pinch of asafoetida
1 bunch of coriander leaves

Dice beetroot; finely chop onion, tomatoes, garlic, and coriander leaves. Boil tamarind in water and squeeze out the juice. Cook chopped beetroot with a glass of water. Cool and purée in a mixer-grinder. Grind black peppercorns and cumin seeds in a mixer-grinder to form a coarse powder.

In a pot, pour in tamarind juice, 2 glasses of water, onions, tomatoes, garlic, turmeric powder, chilli powder, coriander powder, pepper-cumin powder, and salt to taste. Boil for 15 minutes. Then add the beetroot purée and boil for another 5 minutes. Turn off the flame.

In a tempering spoon, heat *ghee* and roast mustard seeds, red chillies broken in half, curry leaves, and a pinch of asafoetida. Once the mustard seeds splutter, turn off the flame and add coriander leaves for a few seconds. Pour this into the *rasam* pot and mix well.

Serve with hot rice or as a soup.

Sumana's Gokarna Kai Rasa

Arunesh Maiyar

Serves 4

TAMARIND PASTE:
A cricket ball-sized ball of tamarind
2 cups water

MASALA:
2 cups grated coconut
1 flat tsp coriander seeds
1 heaped tsp *chana dal*
1 heaped tbsp white sesame seeds
6–8 Byadagi red chillies
A pinch of mustard seeds

STEW:
1 medium-sized pineapple (500 g)
3 tbsp tamarind paste
3–4 tbsp jaggery powder
2–3 cups water
3 tbsp chopped fresh coriander leaves
Salt to taste

TEMPERING:
2 tbsp coconut oil
1 flat tsp mustard seeds
½ tsp turmeric powder
3–4 pinches asafoetida
8–10 fresh curry leaves
2 Byadagi red chillies

Prepare tamarind paste in advance. Take dry tamarind, clean and wash it, and check for grit and fibre. Heat 2 cups of water and bring it to a boil. Add tamarind and wait until it softens and opens out. Transfer to a bowl. Press the tamarind with the back of a fork and keep aside for about 15 minutes. Use a tablespoon to mash the softened tamarind to produce a saucy paste. Strain and keep aside. Store excess paste in an airtight container in the refrigerator (it can be stored upto a week).

For the stew, peel and cut pineapple, remove the central core and fibrous eyes, and cut into 15 ¾-inch dices and keep aside.

To roast the *masala*, heat a tempering spoon and add sesame seeds. Fry evenly till they turn light brown. Some will fly like fleas, let them. Constant stirring helps for even colouring. When done, set aside in a plate to cool. Next, add less than ½ tbsp of coconut oil and roast *chana dal* till reddish-yellow. Watch the flame as the spoon is already hot. Remove the roasted *chana dal* into a fresh plate, but retain oil in the spoon. Spread the *chana dal* to cool faster. Use leftover oil to roast coriander seeds. These colour very fast, so stir constantly. When they turn a deeper brown, take off the flame and mix with the *chana dal*. Next, break Byadagi chillies into roughly 1-inch pieces and add into the tempering spoon. Add more oil only if the spoon is empty. The chillies need to be stirred until they fluff up a bit and become a deeper red—a pigeon blood red. Remove into the plate with *chana dal*. Lastly, roast mustard seeds in the remaining oil. This burns very quickly. Mix the mustard seeds with *chana dal,* coriander seeds, and chillies, and let them cool.

Blend grated coconut in a mixer-grinder, adding ¼ cup of warm water if the coconut is cold from the refrigerator. Add all the cooled spices from the second plate (without the sesame seeds, which will go in last) and adequate room temperature water. Blend to a fine paste. Finish by adding the sesame seeds (sesame seeds are not added earlier as its oil curdles the texture of the coconut paste). Keep this preparation aside.

In a deep, thick-bottomed pan, heat 2 to 3 cups of water. Taste the pineapple for its own share of tartness, as the quantity of tamarind paste will hinge on it. Add most of the tamarind paste and most of the jaggery into the hot water. Check the sweet and sour balance and adjust according to taste. Ideally, it should taste both sweet and sour equally. Add salt to taste. When the water is about to boil, add in cubes of pineapple and let it stew till it is three-quarters cooked. Ensure not to cook the pineapple fully, since it will continue to cook additionally with the *masala* added. Add the ground paste, making sure to rinse out the jar with a little water to get every bit of the paste. This will amplify the volume of the stew.

Cover and let it cook. Add water if required, but without diluting the silken consistency and the rich taste of the gravy. The gravy must be approximately 1 ½ litres now and some water will be lost during boiling. Check salt, tamarind, and jaggery. Cook till the taste of raw coconut is gone and the gravy acquires a satin-silk texture. Chop coriander leaves and add to the gravy and boil for 2 more minutes.

To temper, heat coconut oil in a tempering spoon over a low flame and add 1 tsp of mustard seeds. When it crackles and pops, add ½ tsp of turmeric powder, asafoetida, whole red chillies, and finally curry leaves. Stir gently and let all ingredients blend well in the oil. Pour into the stew and stir. Cover the lid immediately to trap the flavours.

Serve hot with fluffy (not grainy) white rice, accompanied with jackfruit *papad*.

Notes:
—Homemade tamarind paste is preferred but can be substituted with store-bought versions.

—If using a block of jaggery, it should be roughly the volume of a 1½-inch cube. If you have liquid jaggery, 3 tbsp should do.

—The riper the pineapple, the faster it cooks and its texture also softens. In case the pineapple has been overcooked during the boiling stage, strain the preparation and keep aside the pineapple. Add it back into the stew later, after the *masala* has been cooked in the sweet and sour liquid.

—Use finely-chopped (but not ruthlessly fine) fresh coriander leaves, so that they make their motley presence felt in the stew.

—Regarding measurement, use a standard tea cup.

—Rock salt is the rural preference.

—Wooden spoons are ideal for roasting the spices as metal spoons tend to become too hot.

—When roasting, if the sesame seeds get a black lining, discard and start over.

—For tempering, use a deep-bowled long-handled ladle, made of cast iron, stainless steel, or aluminium.

—1 cup of coconut milk can be used as a substitute for the grated coconut. If freshly grated coconut is stored refrigerated, keep outside for an hour to thaw.

Sumana's Gokarna Sambrani

Arunesh Maiyar

Serves 10

400 g raw mango
1 ½ l water

COCONUT MILK:
1 coconut
2 cups water

MASALA:
2 green chillies
5 tbsp coriander leaves
White rock salt to taste

TEMPERING:
½ tbsp coconut oil
½ tsp mustard seeds
1 flat tsp cumin seeds
1 flat tsp asafoetida
2–3 curd chillies
8–10 curry leaves

Start with the *masala*. For this, chop green chillies to ⅓-inch slices (the size is important). Chop coriander leaves, not too fine but not too rough either—a size enough to speckle the *rasam*. For tempering, use 2-inch long curd chillies cut into equal halves.

Slice off the heads of the mangoes, slit in a few places and boil to a pulp in a pressure cooker with ½ a cup of water for two whistles (three if very hard). Open once the steam escapes. If underdone, pressure-cook for one more whistle. Once cooled, peel the skin (if the skin has a lot of pulp, scrape it off with a spoon). Mash the raw mango pulp to a fine paste, either by whisking with a fork or a whisk, or blend in a mixer-grinder and keep aside.

For the coconut milk, grate the coconut and blend it in a mixer-grinder. If the coconut is cold from the refrigerator, add ½ a cup of warm water to prevent curdling. Add one more cup of water and blend till the grated coconut is finely ground. Strain this water. This is the first extract, keep this aside. Now repeat the same exercise with the grated coconut residues by adding another cup of water and blending it once more. Strain this second extract and keep aside separately.

Take a large bowl or pan and add 1 ½ litre of water into it, based on the sourness of the mango pulp at hand. Add most of the mango pulp into the water and stir it well. Taste to check the sourness. If it is too strong, correct the taste by adding water glass by glass. Now add and whisk in the coconut milk, first by adding the first extract. Check for the sweet and sour balance. If the balance is achieved do not use the second extract.

To make the *masala*, take a flat-bottomed stainless steel pan. In the centre of the pan place chopped coriander leaves like a mound slightly flat on the top (like the South African Table Mountain). Place rock salt on it. Finally, place chopped chilli on top of the salt and, using your fingers, crush the chillies through the salt crystals into the chopped coriander till the leaves get a bit lumpy. Now pour the mango and coconut milk liquid into the pan containing the freshly finger-crushed *masala* and stir well.

Heat coconut oil in a tempering spoon and add ingredients in the order listed, allowing each item to splutter before the next is added. When spices crackle and flavors fly in your face, pour into the vessel containing the *sambrani*—the raw mango and coconut *rasam*.

Serve with hot fluffy steamed rice, preferably in a bowl as the runny texture of the *sambrani* does not allow for the fluffy rice grains to absorb its essence.

Notes:
—This recipe is a Gokarna and West Coast summer coolant with raw mango and coconut milk, with fragrances of fresh green chillies and rock salt. It is of Coastal Karnataka and Maharashtrian origin.

—Have this for lunch to offset the effects of the searing April sun by inducing sleep postprandial.

—Kept refrigerated, its soothing effects are soporific.

On ingredients and equipment:
—Choose a young, hard mango for its tartness. Make sure the skin outside is dark green and the flesh inside is white.

—Curd chilli is salt and buttermilk cured desiccated green chilli, available in most supermarkets.

—Rock salt crystals are preferred for the *masala* as they tear into the skin of the chilli while crushing them into heaped coriander leaves—the method mentioned in the recipe.

—While preparing the mango pulp, remember not to open the lid of the pressure cooker till all steam has escaped.

—For extracting the coconut milk, use a robust blender that can pulverize the grated coconut into a fine powder. Some imported blenders don't do the job.

—While straining the ground coconut, use a strainer whose holes are not too small or too large as fine particles of coconut can pass through and ruin the *rasam's* texture.

—Do not exceed 8 to 9 glasses of water in the raw mango pulp while blending, unless the sourness of the pulp can take more water. Remember that the coconut milk will drastically reduce the tartness by bringing its cloying sweetness and grease!

—While preparing the *masala*, use a stainless steel flat bottomed pan, as tartness from the mango may corrode aluminum or Teflon vessels.

—For tempering the spices, use any vegetable oil in place of coconut oil, if preferred.

—This dish can also be served as a drink.

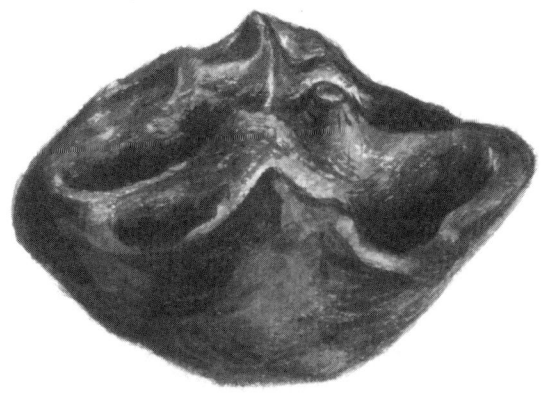

Gauri Lankesh's Urgent Saaru

Pushpamala N

Serves 4

GRAVY:
2 onions
8 tomatoes
7–8 cloves of garlic
1 cup grated coconut
2 tbsp *garam masala*
2 tsp red chilli powder
A marble-sized ball of tamarind
1 tsp salt

TEMPERING:
2 tbsp oil
1 tsp mustard seeds
1 tsp cumin seeds
10 curry leaves

Chop tomatoes and onions. Grind together all the ingredients listed under gravy in a mixer-grinder. Keep aside.

Temper mustard seeds, cumin seeds, and curry leaves in 2 tbsp of oil. Add this to the ground ingredients. Boil the ground and tempered mix in water with 1 tsp of salt until it stops smelling raw.

Serve with hot rice.

Soppu Cream Saaru

(Greens Cream Saaru)

Sheela Gowda

Serves 2

MASALA:
A small bunch of amaranth leaves
¼ cup grated coconut
10–15 black peppercorns
¾ bulb of garlic
A small bunch of coriander leaves
¾-inch piece of tamarind
1 cup water

SAARU:
1½ cup milk
½ tsp jaggery powder
Salt to taste

Cook the greens in a small amount of water, drain, and set aside both.

Add all the other ingredients of the *masala* to the cooked greens and grind to a fine paste in a mixer-grinder. Add the cooked water, salt, and jaggery powder to it and bring it to a boil. Add milk and turn off the heat just as it begins to boil.

Best served hot with rice, *sandige*, or *papad*.

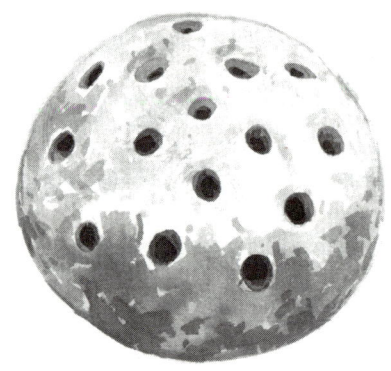

Raw Jackfruit Curry

Renu Appachu

Serves 6

1 medium-sized raw jackfruit
1 cup water

MASALA:
½ cup grated coconut
1 tbsp cumin seeds
A lime-sized ball of tamarind
1 tbsp red chilli powder
1 big onion
4 cloves of garlic
½ tbsp coriander seeds
Salt to taste

TEMPERING:
10 curry leaves
1 tbsp mustard seeds
1 tbsp cooking oil

Skin the jackfruit, remove its flesh, and dice it into small pieces. Keep aside. Finely chop onion and grind together with the other ingredients listed under *masala* into a fine paste.

In a pan over a low flame, add in raw jackfruit pieces, along with the *masala*. Mix well and pour in a cup of water. Stir well and let it cook. Once the jackfruit is tender and the *masala* is cooked, take it off the flame and keep aside.

In a small pan, heat 1 tbsp of oil, and add mustard seeds and curry leaves. Once the mustard seeds pop, take off the flame and add this to the curry.

Serve with boiled rice.

Baimbale Curry

(Bamboo Shoot Curry)

Renu Appachu

Serves 4

500 g fresh bamboo shoots
3 cups water
1 tsp turmeric powder
Salt to taste
3–4 pieces of *kudampuli*

MASALA:
1 big onion
5 cloves of garlic
1 tsp red chilli powder
1 tsp coriander powder
¼ tbsp cumin seeds
1 whole coconut

Separate the layers of the bamboo shoot (like a cabbage) and soak it in water for 24 hours. Following this, drain the water and soak it again for 24 hours. Drain the second water. After this process, it begins to ferment slightly. This preparatory step is very important because bamboo shoots contain arsenic which is poisonous. Chop the shoots into 1-inch pieces.

In a pot, boil bamboo shoots in 3 cups of water till tender, with 1 tsp of turmeric powder and 1 tsp of salt. Drain the water and keep aside.

Finely chop onion and garlic. Grind this into a paste together with the other ingredients listed under *masala*. Soak *kudampuli* in a small vessel of boiling water till it is mushy and keep aside.

In a pan over a low flame, put in the ground *masala* paste and cooked bamboo shoots. Add a little water to the gravy and mix well. Once it is half-cooked, add in the *kudampuli* pulp and its water, salt to taste, and mix well.

Serve hot with rice.

Notes:
—This typical Kodava dish is made in the monsoon when the bamboo shoots are tender and not woody. The shoots are peeled and the tender part is used after an elaborate process.

Pineapple Curry

Suresh Jayaram

Serves 8

2 medium-sized pineapples
1 lime-sized piece of jaggery
2 pinches of asafoetida
1 cup coconut milk
2 tsp oil
1 tsp mustard seeds
100 ml water
Salt to taste

MASALA:
4 dry red chillies
1 tsp fenugreek seeds
1 tsp cumin seeds

Peel and chop pineapples into small cubes.

Heat a pan and dry roast 4 red chillies, fenugreek seeds, and cumin seeds. Let this mixture cool, then grind in a mixer-grinder into a coarse powder.

Heat oil in a pan and add mustard seeds and asafoetida. Once the mustard seeds splutter, add in chopped pineapple with 100 ml of water. Cook till the pineapple is well done and then mash the mixture. Add the prepared *masala* and powdered jaggery, and cook well for 10 minutes. Take it off the heat and let it cool for 2 to 3 minutes. Now add coconut milk and salt to taste.

Serve hot with rice, *roti, dosa,* or bread.

Notes:
—An interesting feature of asafoetida (*hing*) is that it can only be used in hot oil or *ghee*. If put directly on a dish without either, it won't have any effect as it must be fried for its taste to be released. The same goes with other spices such as cumin seeds, mustard seeds etc. With the red chilli, oil or *ghee* has a contrasting effect. It reduces its potency.

Pappu

Raghu Tenkayala

Serves 8

2 cups *toor dal*
10–12 fenugreek seeds
3–4 Guntur chillies
3–4 Byadagi chillies
4–5 cloves of garlic
1 onion
2 tomatoes
A marble-sized ball of tamarind
A pinch of turmeric powder
Salt to taste
1 tbsp oil

TEMPERING:
2 tsp *ghee*
A pinch of mustard seeds
A pinch of cumin seeds
1 tsp *urad dal*
8–10 curry leaves

Finely chop the onion, tomatoes, and garlic. Wash *dal* and keep aside.

In a pressure cooker, add oil and fenugreek seeds, and fry until it becomes golden-brown. Make sure not to burn the seeds. Add onions and garlic and fry until the raw odour disappears. Add chillies (broken in half) and *toor dal*; fry for 2 minutes. Add tamarind, turmeric powder, and tomatoes. Add enough water to cover all the ingredients and salt to taste. Close the lid and cook for three to four whistles. Once the pressure is released, mash the cooked dal to an even consistency—you shouldn't be able to distinguish the various elements. Add a tempering of mustard seeds, cumin seeds, *urad dal*, and curry leaves, fried in *ghee*.

Serve with hot rice and *ghee*.

Notes:
—Do not use more than 10–12 fenugreek seeds as the dish may become too bitter.

—The consistency of this *dal* is meant to be thick; don't add too much water.

Bele Saaru

(Lentil Saaru)

Dr. Hemalatha Bhuvanendra

Serves 4

125 g *toor dal*
2 drumsticks
2 onions
2 tomatoes
A handful of coriander leaves
A ball of tamarind as big as half a lime
½ coconut
1 tsp mustard seeds
A pinch of turmeric powder
1 tsp salt
1 sprig of curry leaves
1 tsp MTR *sambhar* powder
1 glass water
1 tsp oil

Cut drumsticks into 1½-to-2-inch pieces and remove the fibre. Chop onions and tomatoes into medium-sized pieces.

Wash *toor dal* and soak in twice the amount of water. Cook the *dal* in a pressure cooker with a pinch of turmeric powder. After two whistles, turn off the flame and keep aside.

In a mixer-grinder, grind tamarind and coconut along with the *sambhar* powder.

In a pan, add 1 tsp of oil and once hot, add mustard seeds and curry leaves. Once the mustard seeds splutter, add chopped onions and fry till they turn pink. Add in chopped tomatoes and the tamarind-coconut paste. Pour a glass of water and add the boiled *dal* into it. Add drumsticks, 1 tsp of salt, and boil for 15 minutes till the drumsticks are soft. Season with finely-chopped coriander leaves.

Serve hot with rice.

Notes:
—You can also add other vegetables like beans, kohlrabi, carrots, potato, brinjal, and ridge gourd.

—MTR is a popular food products company based in Bangalore.

Bassaaru

Dr. Hemalatha Bhuvanendra

Serves 4

1 bunch green or red amaranth leaves
1 bunch dill leaves
1 bunch mountain spinach
250 g *toor dal*
Salt to taste
Water as required

MASALA:
1 tsp oil
2 cloves of garlic
2 onions
4 green chillies
3 dry red chillies
1 tsp cumin seeds
6 black peppercorns
2 tbsp coriander seeds
½ coconut
A lime-sized ball of tamarind

TEMPERING:
1 tbsp groundnut oil
2 sprigs of curry leaves
1 tsp mustard seeds

Cut the roots off the greens and clean the leaves. Soak them in water for half an hour, wash 2 to 3 times, and keep aside. Finely chop onions, green chillies, and garlic, and grate coconut.

Take a pan with 1 tsp oil. Once hot, add chopped garlic, onions, green and red chillies. Then add cumin seeds, peppercorns, and coriander seeds, and fry till golden-brown. Keep it aside and allow it to cool. Use a mixer-grinder to grind grated coconut, tamarind, and the fried ingredients together to a fine paste.

Take *toor dal* with some water and boil it in the pressure cooker with the ground paste. After the *dal* is half-boiled, add the three varieties of leaves and boil it with salt to taste. Once cooked, heat 1 tbsp of oil in a tempering spoon, add mustard seeds and curry leaves, and add this to the *bassaaru*.

Serve with rice or *roti*.

Notes:
—If the stems of the greens are tender you can use it along with the leaves.

—If the specific greens mentioned in the recipe are not available, the *bassaaru* can be made with any variety of local greens.

3-in-1 Bassaaru, Palya, and Chutney

Sheela Gowda

Serves 4

150 g *toor dal*
250 g flat beans
A bunch of amaranth leaves
A bunch of dill leaves
1 full bulb of garlic
¾ tsp jaggery powder
Salt to taste
2 l water

MASALA FOR BASSAARU:
¼ cup grated coconut
¾ tsp cumin seeds
¾ tsp black peppercorns
5–6 green chillies
1 medium-sized onion
¾ bulb of garlic
¼ tsp jaggery powder
Salt to taste
A bunch of coriander leaves
1-inch piece of tamarind

TEMPERING FOR PALYA:
4 dry red chillies
1 sprig of curry leaves
1 tsp mustard seeds
1 tsp oil

GARNISH FOR PALYA:
¼ cup grated coconut

Cook *toor dal* and flat beans in about 2 litres of water along with cloves of garlic from 1 bulb, a little salt, and ¾ tsp of jaggery powder for 10 minutes, in a large pressure cooker without the lid. Wash and chop amaranth and dill leaves, and add them to the cooker.

Take a tall narrow pot with a stable bottom that will easily sit inside the pressure cooker. Add a cup of the partly-cooked *toor dal* and flat beans along with some of the water (not the greens). Add ½ of the onion (roughly cut), ½ of the garlic cloves, and the green chillies from the ingredients listed under *masala* into this pot. Cover the pot and set it in the centre of the pressure cooker so that it is stable and does not topple while cooking. Make sure the top of the pot is sufficiently above the level of the ingredients already inside the cooker. Cook for three whistles, remove the pot, and allow it to cool. Lightly fry the remaining ½ onion (roughly cut) and ½ of the garlic cloves, and add this to the cooked contents of the narrow pot, along with the rest of the ingredients listed under *masala*. Grind this mixture to a fine paste in a mixer-grinder. Do not add too much salt as the *toor dal* in the cooker already has salt in it.

For the *bassaaru*, empty the contents of the pressure cooker into a colander and collect the drained liquid. Add ¾ of the ground paste into the drained liquid and bring to a light boil. Set aside. No tempering necessary. The extra ground paste can be served separately as a chutney.

For the *palya*, heat a tsp of oil in a tempering pan, add red chillies broken in half, curry leaves, and mustard seeds, and add to the *toor dal,* flat beans, and greens mixture. Garnish with grated coconut.

Serve the *bassaaru* with *ragi mudde* or rice, accompanied by *palya* and chutney.

Notes:
—The 150 g of *toor dal* can be replaced with a mix of half *toor dal* and half horse gram or green gram.

—Flat beans (*chapparadavare*) can be replaced with *thogarikai* (shelled fresh *toor* beans). These can be used along with the lentils when in season, or not at all.

—The lentils and the greens can also be combined with chopped cabbage or with fresh French beans.

—A bit of fresh lime juice or a green chilli added into the *bassaaru* while eating with *ragi mudde* gives it a raw tangy/spicy edge. The chutney can also be mixed in as required while serving.

Avarekai Masale Saaru

(Hyacinth Beans Masale Saaru)

Anita Rao Kashi

Serves 4

2 cups shelled hyacinth beans
Salt to taste
1 cup water

MASALA:
2 medium-sized onions
3 medium-sized tomatoes
½ cup fresh grated coconut
15–20 cloves of garlic
2-inch piece of ginger
A fistful of coriander leaves
5 cloves
2-inch cinnamon stick
1 tsp coriander powder
1 tsp poppy seeds
1 tsp red chilli powder

TEMPERING:
1 medium-sized onion
1 medium-sized tomato
1 bunch of fresh mint leaves
1 tsp mustard seeds
½ tsp turmeric powder
3 tbsp oil

Roughly chop 2 onions and 3 tomatoes. Grind all ingredients listed under *masala* to a smooth paste. Pressure cook hyacinth beans till soft, but not mushy; about three to four whistles.

Finely chop 1 onion and 1 tomato. Heat oil in a wide, thick-bottomed *kadhai*. Add turmeric powder and mustard seeds. When the seeds splutter, add mint leaves, then the finely-chopped onion and tomato. Fry till the raw smell disappears. Add ground *masala* and a cup of water and sauté on a low flame till oil separates; this will take 8 to 10 minutes. Add cooked hyacinth beans (along with its water) and salt, and simmer for about 5 minutes. Remove from fire.

Serve with rice, *ragi mudde, akki rotti,* or wheat *roti*.

Notes:
—This can also be made thicker by not adding water with the ground *masala*.

—*Avarekai* can be substituted with several other ingredients/vegetable combinations, such as brinjal-potato, drumstick-potato, brinjal and soaked whole lentils, mixed soaked whole lentils, mixed sprouts, mixed greens, boiled eggs, etc.

—Another popular version is with sprouted horse gram; while making this version, add 2 tbsp of steamed sprouts while grinding ingredients for the *masala*.

Molake Hulli

(Sprouts Hulli)

Dr. Hemalatha Bhuvanendra

Serves 6

1 cup whole black *chana*
1 cup whole *moong*
1 cup horse gram
500 ml water (2 cups)
Salt to taste

MASALA:
1 tbsp oil
1 bulb of garlic
2 onions
2 tomatoes
A handful of coriander leaves
A handful of grated coconut
A lime-sized ball of tamarind
1 tsp MTR *sambhar* powder

TEMPERING:
1 tsp oil
1 tsp mustard seeds
2 sprigs of curry leaves

Soak *chana*, *moong*, and horse gram in water overnight. Drain and tie the lentils in a piece of cloth, cover it with a vessel, and keep in a dark place for one day. When they start sprouting, take out and wash.

Chop garlic, onions, and tomatoes. Heat 1 tbsp of oil in a pan and add garlic. When it turns golden-brown, add onions and sauté till pink. Then add tomatoes and coriander leaves. Remove from flame and grind with coconut, tamarind, and *sambhar* powder.

Pressure cook sprouts in 2 cups of water for two whistles. Open the pressure cooker lid and cook on low heat. Add the ground *masala* and salt. In a tempering spoon, heat 1 tsp of oil, add mustards seeds and curry leaves. Add the tempering into the sprouts mixture and boil further.

Serve this with rice, *ragi mudde,* or even *chapati* and *papad*.

RICE AND STAPLES

Bhakri ✦ Akki Rotti ✦ Masale Akki Rotti ✦ Ragi Mudde ✦ Kadambuttu ✦ Akki Tari ✦ Coconut Milk Pulao ✦ Sunday Pulao ✦ Menthya Palav ✦ Masale Bath ✦ Chicken Biryani ✦ Asmi Bhabhi's Fish Biryani ✦ Ummima's Jhinge jo Hao

Bhakri

Rucha Vibhute

Makes 4–5 bhakris

2½ cups pearl millet (*baajra*) flour
1 cup hot water
Salt to taste

In a deep pot, add 2 cups of pearl millet flour and salt and make a depression in the middle. Add hot water, little by little, and knead into a soft dough. Make sure the water is hot, as otherwise in the next step the *bhakri* will break. Divide the dough into golf-ball-sized balls. Do not keep the dough aside once kneaded—make the *bhakri* immediately. Dust dry flour over the rolling board and pat the ball of dough on it to make a flat disc 5 to 6 inches in diameter.

Heat a *tawa* and place the disc on it. Make sure the flour dusted side is on top. Turn the flame to low heat. Moisten the top by brushing with water immediately. Once the water dries up, flip the *bhakri* and cook for a minute. Immediately after, cook the un-moistened side directly on the flame for another minute, turning it constantly so that it doesn't burn.

Once ready, serve with curries, pickle, *ghee*, jaggery, sliced onion, *thecha*, curd, and chutney.

Notes:
—Can be made with different flours, including *jowar*—sorghum flour. Different flours can also be combined together, with grated vegetables mixed in, to make *thalipeeth*.

—Sesame seeds can be added on the dry side, once the moistened side is brushed with water.

—*Bhakri* is a staple diet of the agricultural community in Maharashtra, Gujarat, Rajasthan, and also some parts of Karnataka.

Akki Rotti

(Rice Rotti)

Renu Appachu

Makes 12–15 rottis

3 cups overcooked rice
1½ cup rice flour
½ cup water
Salt to taste

Mix cooked rice and 1 cup of rice flour with water and salt, and knead into dough—the consistency of wheat *roti* or bread dough. Make golf-ball-sized balls and using a rolling pin flatten it into circles. Use the rest of the dry rice flour to make sure the dough doesn't stick to the rolling pin or the base.

Roast on a hot *tawa* till it is cooked and fluffs up. Serve with curries.

Notes:
—Can also be made with leftover cooked rice.

Masale Akki Rotti

(Masale Rice Rotti)

Anita Rao Kashi

Makes 8–10 rottis

500 g rice flour
1 cup grated coconut
2 large onions
5–6 green chillies
½ cup coriander leaves
1 tbsp cumin seeds
Salt to taste
50–75 ml cooking oil
2 cups water, or as required

Finely chop onions, green chillies, and coriander leaves.

Take all ingredients, except oil, in a large bowl and mix well. Add water little by little and continue to mix till it comes together as a large ball of stiff dough. Make sure it is really firm; if watery, add more flour and adjust salt. Divide into cricket-ball-sized balls, cover, and keep aside.

Take an aluminium *kadhai* and make sure there is no moisture in it. Pour a spoon of oil and smear till an inch from the edge. Take a ball of dough, place it in the centre, and pat it outwards, gradually increasing the size. Spread it evenly so it is approximately ½ cm thick all over. Make a few holes (one in the centre and four halfway to the edge). Place on medium heat and put a drop of oil in each of the holes and about ½ a tsp around the edge. Cover and cook till the *rotti* comes off the surface of the *kadhai*. This will take 7 to 8 minutes. It will brown and crisp around the centre and remain soft around the edges. Let it stay for a few more minutes if you want it crisper and remove.

Serve with butter/*ghee*, coconut chutney, and tamarind *thokku*.

Notes:
—If there's even a hint of moisture in the *kadhai*, the *rotti* will stick and break.

—To cool down the *kadhai* for making the next *rotti*, hold the overturned *kadhai* under a tap and run water gently to cool it, but ensure no water drips into the *kadhai*.

—If you don't have an aluminium *kadhai*, use a *tawa*. Use non-stick only if you have to; it doesn't brown and crisp properly like how an *akki rotti* should. You can also grease a piece of banana leaf or a sheet of foil to pat the dough into a ½-cm-thick disc and overturn it on a *tawa*. Cover with lid and cook as indicated before.

Variations:
—Along with coriander leaves, add chopped mint leaves, fenugreek leaves, and dill leaves to make greens *akki rotti*.

—To make a veggie-loaded *akki rotti*, mix any or all of these: grated carrot, cucumber, ridge gourd, chayote, potato, radish, and spring onions. But these will shed water, so mix with flour, leave aside for a few minutes and then make the dough. For texture and crunch, add roasted split peanuts.

Ragi Mudde

(Finger Millet Ball)

Dr. Hemalatha Bhuvanendra

Makes 8–10 muddes

2 cups *ragi* flour
1 glass water
A few drops of oil

Pour water into a pot, add a few drops of oil and a spoon of *ragi* flour, and bring it to boil. Add the rest of the *ragi* flour, little by little, stirring constantly with the *mudde kolu,* till it becomes semi-solid—a porridge-like consistency. Once all the flour is incorporated, take the stick out and cover the pot. Let it simmer on a low flame for 5 to 10 minutes. Open the lid every few minutes to make sure that the *ragi* flour isn't burning or sticking.

Once it is cooked, it becomes slightly lighter in colour. To check, take a pea-sized bit and roll between your fingers; if it doesn't stick, it means the flour is cooked. Remove from fire and stir vigorously with the *mudde kolu* until it becomes soft, resembling the consistency of a *halwa*. Empty the contents onto the kitchen platform or a large plate/dish. Dip your hand in water, break off sweet-lime-sized pieces, and knead into balls. This has to be done quickly otherwise it will not come together. Keep dipping your hand in water since it will be quite hot.

Serve with *saaru* and a spoon of *ghee*.

Notes:
—This recipe traditionally requires a *mudde kolu*—a wooden stick specially used to make *ragi mudde*. A handle of a wooden ladle can be used instead.

Kadambuttu

Smitha Cariappa

Makes 12–15 kadambuttus

2 cups rice
2 tsp *ghee*
4 cups water
Salt to taste

Wash and drain rice. In a pan, add 2 cups of rice and 4 cups of water. Add salt to taste and place the pan on high heat. When the water starts to boil, lower the heat and cook, stirring constantly until it reaches the consistency of a soft dough. Scrape the sides, making sure that it doesn't stick and burn. Remove the pan from the fire and let it cook in its own heat for about 10 minutes.

Moisten your palms with *ghee* and while the dough is still hot, pinch lime-sized pieces out and mould them into balls. Steam these in a pressure cooker and remove after one whistle.

This is traditionally served with pork curry, but can also be served for breakfast with honey and chutney.

Notes:
—The dough can be kept for many days and can be steamed before serving.

Akki Tari

Babu Eshwar Prasad

Serves 2

1 cup broken rice
2 cups milk
4 green chillies
1 cup grated coconut
1 onion
1 tsp cumin seeds
2 tsp chopped coriander leaves
Salt to taste

Rinse broken rice in water and drain. Finely chop green chillies and onion. Add these to the drained rice along with grated coconut, cumin seeds, coriander leaves, and salt. Add milk and mix well.

Take a quarter steel plate and grease it with oil. Spread the mix evenly on the plate and steam for 20 minutes in the pressure cooker without the weight. This steaming process is similar to the way one would make *idlis*.

Once ready, *akki tari* can be cut into pieces. It is generally served with coconut chutney.

Notes:
—*Akki tari* is mild and goes well with just about anything.

—A sweet version of *akki tari* is also made often.

—This recipe is from my mother Indira's kitchen. It belongs to her and to the Malnad region where she comes from.

Coconut Milk Pulao

Devi Raju

Serves 8

1 kg rice
2 coconuts
8 glasses water
150 ml cooking oil
4 cinnamon sticks
6 pods of green cardamom
1-inch piece of ginger
1 tsp cloves
1 tbsp turmeric powder
Salt to taste

Soak rice for 10 minutes. Remove coconut from the shell and grind in parts with 6 glasses of water. Strain the fibre out with a strainer. Keep 2 glasses of this thick milk aside and to the other 4 glasses add 2 more glasses of water to dilute it.

In a large pot, pour in oil and once hot, fry cinnamon, cardamom, finely-chopped ginger, and cloves. Add in soaked rice, turmeric powder, and salt. Pour in the large batch of diluted coconut milk, cover, and cook for 10 minutes. After 10 minutes, add in the 2 glasses of thick coconut milk, mix well, and let it cook for another 10 minutes.

Serve hot with curries and side dishes.

Sunday Pulao

Tsohil Bhatia

Serves 3–4

½ cauliflower
1 red onion
2 handfuls of fresh peas
2 tbsp cumin seeds
1 tsp red chilli powder
2 tbsp cooking oil
¼ tbsp pods of green cardamom
¼ tbsp pods of black cardamom
¼ tbsp cloves
¼ tbsp cinnamon sticks
3 handfuls of rice
2 cups water
Salt to taste

Slice the onion and separate the cauliflower into florets.

Heat oil in a pressure cooker or a heavy bottomed pot on a medium flame. Add in cumin seeds and fresh peas, and give them a minute to sizzle. Turn the heat to full and add onions and cauliflower florets, and sauté them for 3 minutes. Add rice and water to the pressure cooker along with salt and red chilli powder. Add green cardamom, black cardamom, cloves, and cinnamon. Cover with lid and wait for three whistles. Let the pressure cooker release steam before you open it, lifting the whistle to check. In case you are using a pot instead of a pressure cooker, let the lid sit on the pot and simmer for 15 minutes.

Serve with a handful of potato chips, mango pickle, and curd on the side.

Notes:
—This recipe is a Sunday staple at my parents' home and gets its name from there. I once prepared it on a lazy Sunday morning as a one-pot comfort meal at 1Shanthiroad for the residents during my time there.

Menthya Palav

(Fenugreek Leaf Pulao)

Sheela Gowda

Serves 4

A big bunch of fenugreek leaves
250–300 g regular white rice, *basmati*, or *jeera* rice
1 cup fresh hyacinth beans
1 bay leaf
2–3 pods of green cardamom
2 cinnamon sticks
2-inch piece of ginger
1 bulb of garlic
1 large onion
6–7 green chillies
A small bunch of coriander leaves
1 cup freshly squeezed coconut milk
2 tbsp oil
1 tsp jaggery powder
Salt to taste

Wash the fenugreek leaves and tender stems, chop, and set aside. Grate ginger and cloves of garlic, finely chop onion and coriander leaves, and slit green chillies lengthwise.

Heat 2 tbsp of cooking oil in a pressure cooker. Once the oil is hot, add bay leaf, cardamom, and cinnamon. Add green chillies and chopped onion, and sauté. Once the onions are cooked, add grated ginger and garlic, and hyacinth beans. Add fenugreek leaves and sauté till its aroma rises. Add chopped coriander.

Wash the rice and add to the cooker, stirring it till it is well mixed with the frying ingredients. Add salt and jaggery. Add the coconut milk along with sufficient water to cook the rice. Cover the cooker and cook for three whistles.

Serve with *ghee*, or *raita* made with curd, chopped tomatoes, onions, and green chillies.

Notes:
—The coconut milk can be replaced with a cup of grated coconut.

—Hyacinth beans are optional, based on their availability.

Masale Bath

(Masale Rice)

Umesh Kumar

Serves 4–5

1½-inch piece of ginger
6 cloves of garlic
4 green chillies
2 onions
½ cauliflower
1 carrot
3 tomatoes
8 French beans
A handful of fresh peas
2 pinches of turmeric powder
250 g rice
750 ml water (or adjust accordingly)
1 tsp salt
3 tbsp oil
1 clove
6–8 black peppercorns
1 pod of green cardamom
½-inch cinnamon stick
3 bay leaves
1 star anise
1 kapok bud (Marathi *moggu*)

GARNISH:
1 sprig of coriander leaves

Grind ginger and garlic into a paste, and finely chop green chillies. Thinly slice onions, chop tomatoes and French beans, separate cauliflower into florets, and dice the carrot.

In a thick-bottomed pot or pressure cooker, heat oil and add clove, peppercorns, cardamom, cinnamon, bay leaves, star anise, and the kapok bud. Add ginger-garlic paste and sauté for a few minutes. Add chillies and onions, and sauté for 5 more minutes. Add tomatoes, beans, carrots, and peas and sauté till they are well done. Then add turmeric powder and sauté for a couple of minutes. Add water and mix well. Once the water comes to a boil, add rice, cauliflower florets, and salt. Stir well, cover and cook for 20 minutes. If the rice is not cooked, add a little water and let it simmer till the rice is well cooked.

Garnish with finely-chopped coriander leaves and serve hot with *raita* or curd.

Chicken Biryani

Bharathesh GD

Serves 8–10

1kg chicken with skin

MARINADE:
6 green chillies
12 mint leaves
2 tbsp fresh ginger-garlic paste
½ tbsp turmeric powder
2 limes
Salt as required

TEMPERING:
8 onions
100 ml cooking oil
6–8 cloves
2-inch cinnamon stick
2 star anise
2 green chillies

MASALA:
20–22 mint leaves
2 tsp red chilli powder
1 tbsp coriander powder
½ tbsp cumin powder
4 tbsp *ghee*
Salt to taste

RICE:
750 g *basmati* rice
4 bay leaves
½ tbsp mace
2 tbsp *shahi jeera*

FLAVOURING:
100 ml milk
A pinch of saffron
½ tbsp fresh nutmeg powder
1 tsp turmeric power
2 tbsp rose water
½ tbsp *kewra* water
3–4 tbsp lime juice

SEALING DOUGH:
50 g refined wheat flour
50 g wheat flour

Wash chicken and drain. Marinate with salt, turmeric, juice of 2 limes, chopped green chillies, mint leaves, and ginger-garlic paste. Refrigerate for 2 hours.

Cut 7 onions into long thin slices, finely chop 1 onion, and slit green chillies. In a large thick-bottomed pot, heat oil and fry the thinly-cut onions until they turn golden-brown, and keep aside. In the same pot, add 100 ml of cooking oil. Once hot, add cloves, cinnamon, star anise, green chillies, and the finely-chopped onion. Fry this for a minute and add marinated chicken. Cook for 5 minutes and then add mint leaves. Then, add red chilli powder, coriander powder, cumin powder, and salt to taste. Stir well and add 2 tbsp of *ghee*. Turn the heat down to a low flame, cover the pot with a lid, and cook for 20 to 25 minutes.

Wash the rice twice and soak for 10 minutes. Heat 2 tbsp of *ghee*, bay leaves, mace, *shahi jeera*, and salt to taste in a big pot on a low flame. Add the soaked rice with twice the amount of water and cook for 8 to 10 minutes or till parboiled.

In a separate bowl, take 100 ml of milk; add a pinch of saffron, nutmeg powder, turmeric powder, rose water, and *kewra* water. Mix well and keep it aside.

Once the chicken is cooked and rice parboiled, transfer half the chicken gravy into a separate vessel. On the leftover chicken gravy in the pot, add a layer of parboiled rice and sprinkle half the fried onions. Then layer the remaining chicken gravy and another layer of rice, and top with remaining fried onions. Use a ladle to pierce a few holes through the layers and pour in the milk preparation and a few tbsps of lime juice into it. Knead refined wheat flour and wheat flour into dough with a little water. Close the pot with a lid and seal this with the dough. Cook it one last time for 10 minutes on a low flame.

Serve hot with *raita*.

Notes:
—This *biryani* can also be prepared with different meats.

—If it is too spicy, squeeze in a lime.

Asmi Bhabhi's Fish Biryani

Bilal Javeed

Serves 4

500 g seer fish (king fish)
2 tsp coconut oil or *ghee*

MARINADE:
1 tsp red chilli powder
¾ tsp turmeric powder
¼ tsp salt
½ tsp *garam masala*
½ tsp cumin powder
1 whole lime
A few curry leaves
1 tsp ginger-garlic paste

MASALA:
2 onions
2 tomatoes
3 green chillies
10 shallots
1 tsp ginger-garlic paste
½ lime
¼ tsp turmeric powder
½ tsp *garam masala*
½ tsp red chilli powder
Salt to taste
½ tbsp coriander leaves
1 sprig of curry leaves
2 tbsp curd

RICE:
2 cups *basmati* rice
3–4 tbsp *ghee*
1 cinnamon stick
2 pods of green cardamom
3 cloves
2 tsp salt
½ lime
4 cups hot water

GARNISH:
1 sprig of coriander leaves

1 onion
A handful of cashew nuts
1 tbsp oil
1 tbsp *ghee*

Marinate fish with the ingredients listed under marinade for 15 minutes. Shallow-fry in coconut oil. Keep aside.

Blend shallots, tomatoes, and green chillies to create a paste. Finely chop onions, coriander leaves, and curry leaves. In a medium-sized pan, add *ghee* or coconut oil and sauté onions till brown. Then add the prepared paste and cook until the water from the paste reduces. Add ginger-garlic paste, lime, turmeric powder, *garam masala*, chilli powder, and salt, and cook for a few minutes. Next, add coriander leaves, curry leaves, and curd. Then add the fried fish and mix thoroughly. Cover and cook on low flame for 10 minutes.

Wash rice and keep aside. In a pressure cooker, add *ghee* and temper the cinnamon, cardamom, and cloves for a minute. Add washed *basmati* rice and mix for a few seconds. Add in hot water, salt, and lime. Pressure cook for two whistles.

In the serving container, layer fish *masala* and rice. Garnish with coriander leaves, onions sliced and fried in oil, and cashews fried in *ghee*.

Serve with *raita*, pickle, and *papad*.

Notes:
—This recipe originally comes from my sister-in-law's mother, who was a fantastic cook. Growing up in coastal Fort Kochi, this recipe was an alternative to the traditional mutton or chicken *biryani* which was prepared every Friday after prayers.

—As an alternative to seer fish, mahi-mahi, barramundi, halibut, or yellowfin tuna can be used for this *biryani*.

Ummima's Jhinge jo Hao

(Ummimaa's Prawn Rice)

Nihaal Faizal

Serves 4

1 onion
2–3 green chillies
2 tbsp ginger-garlic paste
1½ tsp red chilli powder
¾ tsp turmeric powder
½ tsp coriander powder
4–5 fennel seeds
2 tbsp coconut oil
500 g prawns
½ cup curd
½ cup coconut milk
1½ cups rice
2 cups water
Salt to taste

Roughly chop onion and green chillies, and grind into a paste, together with ginger-garlic paste, chilli powder, turmeric powder, coriander powder, and fennel seeds. Wash the rice and keep aside.

Heat oil in a pressure cooker. Once hot, fry the paste. After a few minutes, add curd and stir well. Add in the prawns. When the prawns are half-cooked, add salt and mix well. Quickly add rice, water, and coconut milk; stir and pressure cook for one whistle.

Serve hot with *papad*.

Notes:
—This recipe is a simple one-pot meal that used to be prepared by my great grandmother Fathima Abdullah, who adapted a traditional Kutchi Memon recipe to suit the coastal flavours of Kerala. This recipe was taught to me over the phone by her daughter and my *nani*, Tasneem Arif. Clarifications were later sought from my mother, Zarine Faizal.

ACCOMPANIMENTS

Vegetable Stir-fry ✦ Potato Stir-fry ✦ Beetroot Palya ✦ Quick Thondekai Palya ✦ Padavalanga Thoran ✦ Achinga Mezhukkupuratti ✦ Achinga Mezhukkupuratti with a Twist ✦ Spinach Sabzi ✦ Raw Banana Poriyal ✦ Sweet Potato Poriyal ✦ Ridge Gourd with Peanut Masala ✦ Tamilian Brinjal Masala ✦ Sumana's Bendekai Palya ✦ Sumana's Bendekai Saasme ✦ Pithala ✦ Nellikai Tambli ✦ Curd Curry

Vegetable Stir-fry

Suresh Jayaram

Serves 4

2 red capsicums
1 green capsicum
1 onion
2 large carrots
8–10 button mushrooms
6–8 baby corns
1 tsp ginger-garlic paste
2 tsp sesame seeds
½ tsp black pepper powder
4 tbsp olive oil
1 tbsp salt

Slice capsicums into thin strips—the combination of red and green capsicums is to add a touch of colour to the recipe. Finely chop onion, carrots, mushrooms, and baby corn. The smaller they are cut, the faster they will cook.

Heat oil in a large wok until it smokes, and add sesame seeds. Add chopped onion, ginger-garlic paste, and pepper. Stir till the onion turns brown. Keep stirring to make sure the ginger-garlic paste doesn't stick to the pan. Add carrots and cook till they are half-done. Add capsicum and baby corn, sauté until they are tender. Finally, add mushrooms and sauté for another 2 minutes. Make sure not to overcook the vegetables to retain their crunchiness. Cover the stir-fry and turn off the heat. Add salt before serving.

Serve as a side dish.

Notes:
—When sautéing, put the hardest vegetable first, since it will take the most time to cook.

Variations:
—To the stir-fried vegetables, add a cup of water, mixed with 1 tsp corn starch, to make into a curry. This can be served on a bed of rice or alongside a noodle soup.

—Add dry red chillies and soy sauce for an alternative version.

—If there is leftover stir-fry, mix with cooked rice, soy sauce, and chilli sauce, over a low-flame, to make a fried rice. An addition of scrambled egg is optional.

Potato Stir-fry

Suresh Jayaram

Serves 3

500 g baby potatoes
½ tsp crushed black peppercorns
2 tsp sunflower oil
2 tbsp sesame seeds
A small bunch of dill leaves
1 tsp salt

Finely chop dill leaves and keep aside. Boil cleaned, but unpeeled, baby potatoes in water with 1 tsp of salt. If boiling in a pressure cooker, wait for one whistle. Otherwise wait until the potatoes are firm, but cooked.

Heat oil in a pan over a low flame. When it starts to smoke, add in sesame seeds. Stir until they pop and then take off the flame and cover with a lid. When the popping stops, add in chopped dill leaves and peppercorns. Drain the potatoes and add them into the pan. Return to a low flame. Stir well and add more salt if needed.

Serve as a starter or side dish.

Notes:
—Large potatoes can also be used instead of baby potatoes. In this case, cut in half before boiling.

—Sunflower oil can be substituted with olive or peanut oil.

Beetroot Palya

Dr. Hemalatha Bhuvanendra

Serves 4

3 medium-sized beetroots
2 small onions
4 green chillies
A few curry leaves
A bunch of coriander leaves
½ tsp mustard seeds
1 tsp *chana dal*
1 tsp *urad dal*
1 tsp sunflower oil
Salt to taste
2–3 tsp water

Finely chop onions, coriander leaves, and beetroot. Slit green chillies. Keep these aside.

Heat oil in a pan over a low flame and add mustard seeds. When they splutter, add *chana* and *urad dal*, and fry until they turn golden-brown. Then, add chopped onions and fry till they turn pink. Add green chillies, curry leaves, and beetroot, along with 2 or 3 tsp of water. Cook for 10 to 15 minutes till beetroot becomes tender. Add salt to taste and garnish with coriander leaves.

Serve as a side dish with rice.

Quick Thondekai Palya

(Quick Ivy Gourd Palya)

Jayasimha Chandrashekar

Serves 4

500 g ivy gourd
1 tbsp salt
½ tbsp red chilli powder

TEMPERING:
1 tbsp cumin seeds
1 tbsp mustard seeds
½ tsp turmeric powder
A pinch of asafoetida
3–4 tbsp oil

Wash ivy gourd and pound till it is roughly smashed. Marinate with 2 tbsp of salt and let it sit for 15 minutes. After marination, squeeze the ivy gourd to remove excess water and salt, and keep aside.

Heat oil in a pan, add cumin seeds, mustard seeds, turmeric powder, and asafoetida. Once the mustard seeds splutter, add the ivy gourd and sauté till it is well roasted. Once it is nearly done, add red chilli powder, mix well, and cook for another 5 to 7 minutes.

Serve with hot rice and curry/*dal*.

Padavalanga Thoran

(Snake Gourd Thoran)

Omana Eappen

Serves 4

1 large snake gourd
1 medium-sized onion
3 tbsp grated coconut
2 green chillies
A pinch of turmeric powder
2 tsp coconut oil
½ tsp mustard seeds
5–6 curry leaves
Salt to taste

Peel skin of the snake gourd and remove the seeds inside. Then chop into small cubes or, alternatively, grate it. Finely chop onion and slit green chillies.

Heat coconut oil in a wok over a low flame and add mustard seeds. When they begin to pop, add curry leaves and the chopped onion. Once the onion turns translucent, add chopped snake gourd and turmeric powder. Sauté for a few minutes on a low flame and then add grated coconut. Add salt to taste and keep stirring until it is nearly cooked and tender. Just before finishing, raise to a high flame for just a minute and then take off the fire.

Serve as a side dish with rice.

Notes:
—If the snake gourd does not fully cook while sautéing, add a little water and cover the wok with a lid for a few minutes (before the last step of raising to a high flame).

Achinga Mezhukkupuratti

(Snake Beans Mezhukkupuratti)

Sandeep TK

Serves 6–8

1 kg snake beans
4 tomatoes
3 small onions
3 tbsp sunflower oil
150 ml curd
A handful of curry leaves
2 tbsp red chilli powder
1 tbsp salt
1 tsp turmeric powder
½ cup water

Wash snake beans with salt and turmeric powder, and chop them into 2-to-3-inch pieces. Finely chop onions and tomatoes. Mix these in a container. Add chilli powder, salt, and 2 tbsp oil into the container and mix well. Keep this aside.

Add 1 tbsp of oil into a large pan over a medium flame. When heated, add the contents of the container into the pan and pour about ½ a cup of water. Cook for about 25 minutes over a low flame, until all the water has evaporated. Add curd and curry leaves, and cook for another 10 minutes. This is a recipe that is meant to be overcooked—the overcooking will make it melt in your mouth.

Serve as a side dish with rice or *roti*.

Achinga Mezhukkupuratti with a Twist

(Snake Beans Mezhukkupuratti with a Twist)

Rohini Sen

Serves 4

350 g snake beans
12 shallots
1 large tomato
5 cloves of garlic
1-inch piece of ginger
A sprinkle of brown sugar
¼ tsp cumin powder

MARINADE:
1 tsp turmeric powder
½ tsp red chilli powder
Salt to taste
½ cup water

TEMPERING:
5 tbsp coconut oil
1 tbsp mustard seeds
A hearty pinch of asafoetida
2 sprigs of fresh curry leaves
2 long Byadagi chillies

GARNISH:
A handful of fresh coriander leaves

Chop snake beans into 2-inch pieces, dice shallots, and chop tomato lengthwise. Crush garlic cloves and grate ginger. Dry roast cumin powder and keep aside.

Make a paste with turmeric powder, chilli powder, salt, and a little water. In a large bowl, marinate chopped beans, tomato, and half the chopped shallots with this paste.

While the vegetables are marinating, heat coconut oil in a flat-bottomed pan and wait till the aroma is wafting through your kitchen. Add mustard seeds and allow them to splutter. If you do not employ the virtue of patience and wait for this, chances are that your dish is doomed. Add a pinch of asafoetida and 1 sprig of curry leaves, torn up slightly. Add Byadagi chillies and sauté vigorously so that the chillies do not blacken. Add the other half of the shallots (which have not been marinated) into the pan. Sprinkle brown sugar to speed up the browning of the onions. Once the onions begin to look like translucent brown glass, add crushed garlic and grated ginger, and wait for the raw smell to disappear. Add a little more coconut oil if it seems too dry. Add roasted cumin powder and the marinated beans, tomatoes, and shallots. Cover and cook on medium flame for 5 to 8 minutes, checking to make sure it does not overcook. Check for salt and add some if needed. Add the remaining curry leaves. Turn off the flame when the beans are just about *al dente* (as the Italians say).

Garnish with finely-chopped coriander and serve as a side dish with rice or fluffy *roti*.

Notes:
—The shallots can be replaced with 1 big red onion.

—The large mustard seeds are preferred as they give a nutty zing.

—To make it spicier, you could use a combination of crushed chilli and coarsely crushed black pepper or add 1 chopped green chilli along with the ginger and garlic.

—If it gets too spicy, add ¼ cup of thick coconut cream just before turning off the flame. That usually simmers the heat down but will of course alter the taste considerably.

—I learnt how to make this dish by watching Sandeep TK make it in 1Shanthiroad, and added my own Bengali touch to it!

Spinach Sabzi

Devi Raju

Serves 5

2 bunches of spinach
2 onions
1 tsp mustard seeds
4 cloves of garlic
3 green chillies
½ tsp cumin seeds
¼ cup grated coconut
1 cup *moong dal*
1 tsp sunflower oil
Salt to taste

Soak *moong dal* for half an hour and then drain. Wash spinach thoroughly, finely chop onions, and slit green chillies.

Heat oil in a pan over a medium flame. Add mustard seeds, garlic, green chillies, and cumin seeds, and fry for about 2 minutes. Add onions and cook until soft. Add soaked *moong dal* and grated coconut, and continue to fry for another 2 minutes. Finally, add spinach and salt to taste. Mix well and cover with a lid. Cook this over a slow flame for 10 to 15 minutes.

Serve as a side dish with rice or *roti*.

Raw Banana Poriyal

Ramalingam VK

Serves 4–6

6 raw bananas
½ tsp turmeric powder
Salt to taste
½ coconut

MASALA:
100 g peanuts
6 dry red chillies
1 tbsp coriander seeds
1 tsp mustard seeds
1 tsp cumin seeds
1 tbsp coconut oil

TEMPERING:
4 tbsp coconut oil
1 tsp mustard seeds
2 tsp *urad dal*
A pinch of asafoetida
A handful of curry leaves

First prepare the *masala*. For this, dry roast coriander seeds, mustard seeds, cumin seeds, red chillies, and peanuts separately as they roast at different speeds. Once they cool, grind them together in a mixer-grinder along with 1 tbsp of coconut oil, until it becomes a coarse powder.

Grate coconut and keep aside. Then peel raw bananas and slice them into discs. Boil bananas in water with a pinch of salt and turmeric powder until they are soft but firm. Drain and run them through cold water to prevent them from getting too soft and mushy. Keep aside.

Heat 4 tbsp of coconut oil in a pan and add mustard seeds. When they begin to splutter, add *urad dal*, asafoetida, and curry leaves, in this order. Add boiled bananas and then the ground *masala*. Toss until the bananas are crisp. Garnish with the grated coconut and check for seasoning.

Serve hot with rice and *rasam* or *dal*.

Sweet Potato Poriyal

Ramalingam VK

Serves 4–6

1 kg sweet potatoes
4 tbsp sunflower oil
4 dry red chillies
2 tsp mustard seeds
2 tsp *urad dal*
½ tsp turmeric powder
1 tsp red chilli powder
2 sprigs of curry leaves
Salt to taste

Boil sweet potatoes in water. Peel and cut into 1-inch cubes. Heat oil in a pan over low flame and add mustard seeds, *urad dal*, red chillies, and curry leaves, in this order. Mix well and add sweet potato. Then add turmeric powder, red chilli powder, and salt. Cook on a low flame for 8 to 10 minutes, until the sweet potato develops a golden crispy crust. The crust will be the result of the sugar content in the sweet potato that caramelizes.

Serve hot with rice or *roti,* or as a snack.

Ridge Gourd with Peanut Masala

Ayisha Abraham

Serves 2

2 large ridge gourds
2 small tomatoes
½ cup peanut powder
½ tsp coriander powder
1 tsp turmeric powder
Red chilli powder to taste
Salt to taste
2 tbsp oil
1 tbsp cumin seeds

Cut ridge gourds into finger-length pieces and cook till soft. In a mixer-grinder, grind tomatoes and mix in peanut powder, coriander powder, turmeric powder, red chilli powder, and salt to make a wet paste.

Heat oil in a *kadhai* and add cumin seeds. Once they brown, add the wet paste and fry till the raw smell is gone. Then add cooked ridge gourd pieces, cover, and cook till the paste and vegetable are well done.

Serve hot with *roti* or steamed rice.

Notes:
—Ridge gourd can be replaced with ash gourd, brinjal (slit), or chayote.

—This Marwari recipe is courtesy Ranjana who lives in the rainforest of Coorg with her son and daughter-in-law, and runs an organic farm and homestay.

Tamilian Brinjal Masala

Devi Raju

Serves 4

250 g small round brinjals
2 onions
2 tbsp ginger-garlic paste
½ tsp turmeric powder
1 tsp red chilli powder
3 tsp coriander powder
1 tbsp salt
1 cup water
4–5 curry leaves
1 tsp *garam masala*
A lime-sized ball of jaggery
A lime-sized ball of tamarind
3 tbsp oil

MASALA:
3 tbsp peanuts
1 tbsp cumin seeds
1 tbsp fenugreek seeds
1 tsp black peppercorns
2 onions

Soak the ball of tamarind in hot water and squeeze out the juice. Set aside. Cut brinjals into 4 pieces each; finely chop 2 onions and chop the other 2 into 4 pieces each.

Heat 2 tbsp oil in a pressure cooker, and add finely-chopped onions and ginger-garlic paste. After the onion turns pink, add brinjal, followed by turmeric powder, chilli powder, coriander powder, and salt. Cook for 10 minutes.

While this cooks, heat 1 tbsp oil in a separate pan and add peanuts, cumin seeds, fenugreek seeds, peppercorns, and the 2 remaining onions. Roast this mixture and then grind it into a paste in a mixer-grinder.

To the pressure cooker, add a cup of water, the ground paste, curry leaves, *garam masala*, and jaggery. Cook for 10 more minutes and add the juice of the tamarind and salt to taste. Mix well and remove from fire.

Serve hot as a side dish with rice or *roti*.

Sumana's Bendekai Palya

(Sumana's Okra Palya)

Arunesh Maiyar

Serves 4

500 g okra
½ tbsp tamarind paste
½ tsp jaggery powder
A few sprigs of coriander leaves
Salt to taste

MASALA:
¾ tsp mustard seeds
½ coconut
3–4 Byadagi chillies

TEMPERING:
1½ tsp coconut oil
1 flat tsp mustard seeds
1 flat tsp *urad dal*
¼ tsp turmeric powder
8–10 curry leaves
A pinch of asafoetida

Grate coconut. If it has been refrigerated, keep outside for 30 minutes before use. Portion out the *masala* and tempering ingredients and keep them ready. Wash, towel dry, and lop the heads off the okra—I use them with the tails. Chop them into ½-inch slices.

To make the *masala*, powder mustard seeds to a fine consistency. Then add Byadagi chillies and blend to a fine powder. Lastly, add very little water and freshly grated coconut. Grind this mixture to produce a final coarse texture which has the consistency of a chutney.

For the tempering, heat coconut oil in a thick-bottomed wok or a slightly deep pan. Once hot, introduce the following ingredients in this order. Mustard seeds go in first; wait till they crackle and then add *urad dal*, and allow it to turn slightly blond. Next add turmeric powder and asafoetida. Stir once before adding the curry leaves. Ensure that the spices do not char. Lower the flame or remove while adding successive ingredients if you suspect charring of the spices.

Now to this, add chopped okra, some salt, and stir in the tempered spices well for two rounds. Lower the flame and close the lid for it to steam and cook. Keep checking every 2 minutes, stirring gently so as to not smash the okra. Add a tbsp of water, only if necessary, to prevent burning. Keep the lid closed to steam well. Once half-cooked, add tamarind paste and jaggery, and fold it gently. When the okra is nearly steamed, add the coconut and mustard *masala*. Again, fold it gently, preventing any mashing of the okra. Check for tamarind and salt balance, correcting it if necessary. Steam for another 2 minutes with the lid closed.

Garnish with freshly chopped coriander and serve as a side dish with *roti* or rice.

Notes:
—This is traditionally served with fluffy steamed rice but it goes well with *roti* or *poori*. It can also be served as a topping on French bread or as a filling in a toasted sandwich.

—Procure tender okra with its mild furs visible.

—If using liquid jaggery, add 1 tsp of it for this recipe.

—Please use fresh coriander and curry leaves.

—If you prefer a fainter mustard flavour, just add ½ tsp of mustard seeds in the *masala*.

—Do not use coconut milk as a substitute for the grated coconut in this dish. A coarsely ground coconut texture is crucial here.

Variations:
—Substitute the okra with 2 medium-sized raw bananas (about 400 g). The bananas should be peeled and diced to ¾-cm pieces and then soaked in water. Soaking it in water prevents

the blackening of the edges due to oxidation. You may add 3 tbsp of coconut oil in the tempering to give the dish a crumb fried texture.

—Raw banana stem is another variation—cut into ¼-inch dices after removing its fibre.

—Other variations are with shredded cabbage, brinjals (especially the long parrot-green ones), ivy gourd (*thondekai* in Kannada), chayote, and cluster beans (*gorikai* in Kannada).

Sumana's Bendekai Saasme

(Sumana's Okra Saasme)

Arunesh Maiyar

Serves 4

250 g okra
1 coconut
500 ml curd
1 flat tsp mustard seeds
1½ tbsp *ghee*
Salt to taste
Water as required

MASALA:
3 green chillies
3 tbsp chopped coriander leaves
Rock salt to taste

TEMPERING:
1½ tbsp *ghee*
½ flat tsp mustard seeds
¾ tsp cumin seeds
2 Byadagi chillies
¼ tsp asafoetida
10 curry leaves

Keep curd out of the refrigerator 2 hours prior to cooking to get a mildly sour tinge. Grate a coconut to produce 1 firmly-packed cup and keep aside. If you do not have the typical South Indian round serrated scraper, then remove fresh coconut from the shell, chop, and blend in a mixer-grinder. Wash and dry okra and lop the heads off. Chop into ⅓-cm slices. Chop green chillies into ½-cm slices and Byadagi chillies into ¾-cm slices. Roughly chop coriander leaves.

Heat a flat-bottomed frying pan and pour *ghee*. Wait till it melts. When hot, add chopped okra and sauté for a minute on high flame, stirring constantly. Lower the flame, add salt (just enough to mildly flavour it as the bulk of the salt will be added while making the *masala*) and let it fry. Add a few drops of either *ghee* or coconut oil occasionally to ensure an even crisp frying. It should be crunchy crisp but not be fried to a crackle as then it may disintegrate in the curd when finally immersed. When done, allow it to cool.

While the okra is frying, blend the following ingredients in a medium mixer-grinder jar: first powder mustard seeds, then add grated coconut and some water. Start with 30 ml of warm water in case the grated coconut was refrigerated. Add just enough water to achieve a smooth fluid pulp—not runny, but not as firm as chutney either. Blend ruthlessly to a fine paste. Keep aside.

For the *masala*, take either a final serving dish or a stainless steel bowl and arrange the chopped coriander at the bottom like a mound. Flatten the top and place the chopped chillies on it. Now add the salt on top of the bed of chillies, and crush it down into the chillies and coriander by pressing and mixing with your fingertips till the salt crystals cut through the skin of the green chillies and mix with the heady juices of coriander. You will be left with a very roughly crushed mixture. To this *masala* mix, add the blended mustard and grated coconut paste and mix well. Now blend the curd evenly with a whisk or a fork, and add. To this, add the crunchy crisp okra.

For the tempering, heat *ghee* in a tempering spoon. When you begin to feel the heat, lower the flame and add in this order: mustard seeds, once it begins to crackle, add cumin seeds, red chillies, asafoetida, and finally curry leaves. Each of the ingredients must lose the colour of its rawness but not blacken. Increase the flame as more ingredients fill up the tempering spoon. Add the tempering to the bowl and mix well.

Refrigerate before serving. Serve with hot, fluffy (please note, not grainy) steamed rice. I have it with *roti* too.

Notes:
—A brief note on the generic dishes that are called *saasme*: *saasme* is the coastal Kannada word for mustard seeds. In the South Kanara district of coastal Karnataka, where Udupi is the gourmet capital, this dish employs mustard seeds as one of its taste-forming ingredients. However, in Gokarna, in the North Kanara district, which is my ancestral home town, mustard is used only when okra *saasme* is made.

—Please use all fresh ingredients for this recipe.

—In the *masala*, powdered salt is okay too.

—As a substitute for grated coconut, you could make use of ½ a cup of coconut milk.

—Coconut oil can be used as a substitute for *ghee*.

—Make use of fresh green chillies, quantity varies for mild and sharp ones, so please check. These should be chopped into ½-cm slices, so that little children can identify it when eating and separate it if needed.

—Asafoetida, if crystal, crush and use. L.G. is a popular brand.

—While crushing salt through the chillies and coriander, ensure it does not result in a pulverised paste. Also please note that the fried okra also has salt, so remember to add just the required amount. Now don't stick your fingers anywhere to avoid unmentionable consequences. The chilli silly!

—To prevent burning of the spices, it is best to keep all the ingredients at hand. Managing the heat is very important as spices with fragile constitutions and varying heating points can burn and ruin the dish as this is the last stage of the preparation. *Ghee* can retain a huge amount of latent heat.

Variations:

—Brinjal: The Punjabi *baingan* (*bharta-walla*), the huge purple blobbed teardrops! Roast it on an open flame, remove skin, and chop. Cool before adding it in the last stage, as in the case of the okra. I add a bit of mustard to the coconut when making *saasme* with brinjal, even though *Gokarnakars* may disapprove.

—Chayote (*chow chow*): Peel the vegetable, cut into halves after deseeding it, and pressure cook up to two whistles (three if not very tender) with a cup of water. Cool, mash, and add when the okra is added in the main recipe above. You could also chop it into ½-cm cubes instead of mashing it. I prefer the two halves cooked and then mashed. For this variation use 2 medium-sized chayotes not exceeding 400 g. This has a very tender and homespun flavour of coolness and comfort. A real surprise!

—Cucumber: Grated with skin, partially steamed, and cooled. If you do not have a steamer, place the grated cucumber in a pan after draining off the water (don't squeeze it tight). Add ½ a glass of water. Close the lid of the pan and heat on a low flame. You can drink the cucumber water or add it in your vodka when cooled!

—Spring onions: Finely-chopped and steamed like the cucumber, 1 ½ cup.

—Ridge gourd: Peeled, chopped and boiled, cooled, and added last as above.

—Red pumpkin: De-skinned, grated, and pressure cooked with one whistle.

—Raw banana: De-skinned and pressure cooked whole for two or three whistles depending upon tenderness, mashed, and added to the coconut paste.

—Mangalore cucumber: Grated and pressure cooked for two whistles.

—Carrots and beetroot: Grated and steamed to lose their hardness. Please choose 450 g of juicy carrots and fresh beetroots as they dry up a bit after steaming. The thickening agent here is not grated coconut, but roasted peanuts. Use ½ a cup. Buy unsalted fresh ones, roast till the skin chars, cool, and crush coarsely.

—Potatoes: Boiled and used without the coconut, but with all other elements of *masala* and tempering. This is a good last minute way to turn the tables!

Pithala

Rucha Vibhute

Serves 2–3

1½ cup gram flour
1 tsp mustard seeds
1 tsp cumin seeds
5–8 green chillies
4 tbsp cooking or peanut oil
¼ tsp asafoetida powder
¼ tsp turmeric powder
6 cloves of garlic
5–6 curry leaves
A bunch of coriander leaves
3½ cups water
Salt to taste

Pound garlic, green chillies, and some coriander leaves roughly in a mortar and pestle (or grind in a mixer-grinder) and keep it aside. Chop the rest of the coriander leaves.

In a pan, heat 4 tbsp of oil and add mustard seeds, cumin seeds, asafoetida, turmeric powder, curry leaves, and the garlic-chilli-coriander paste. Stir-fry for 1 to 2 minutes and add 3½ cups of water. Let it come to a boil and then add chopped coriander leaves and salt. Slowly add gram flour in small quantities and keep stirring. Ensure that there are no lumps. Once all the flour is mixed in, cover the pan, and let it cook for 5 minutes till it thickens to the consistency of pancake batter.

Serve it with wheat *chapati, jowar, baajra,* or rice flour *bhakri* along with sliced onion, *thecha (*green chilli chutney), and curd.

Notes:
—Mostly a staple diet of the agricultural community.

—One of the tricks to avoid lumps is to mix the gram flour with water beforehand and then add it to the pan.

—Can be made with horse gram flour instead of gram flour (*besan*).

—Kokum extract and red chilli powder can be used for a sour-spicy flavour.

—Spinach or fenugreek leaves can also be added.

Nellikai Tambli

(Indian Gooseberry Tambli)

Archana Hande

Serves 2

2 Indian gooseberries
½ cup curd
¼ cup fresh grated coconut
3–4 black peppercorns
¼ tsp cumin seeds
Salt to taste

TEMPERING:
½ tsp *ghee*
½ tsp mustard seeds
A pinch of asafoetida
5–6 curry leaves

Grate gooseberries and keep aside. Heat a pan and add a bit of *ghee*. When hot, add cumin seeds, curry leaves, asafoetida, and peppercorns. Fry till cumin seeds turn brown. Grind this with the grated gooseberry. Mix curd, grated coconut, and salt.

For tempering, heat the rest of the *ghee* and add mustard seeds, curry leaves, and asafoetida. Pour into the *tambli* and mix well.

Serve as a side dish with rice or *roti*.

Notes:
—*Tambli* is a south Karnataka dish from Mangalore and Udupi. It can be pronounced as *tambli* or *tambuli*. It is a simple yogurt and coconut based gravy made using raw or lightly sautéed spices or green leafy herbs and vegetables, with little or no spice. It is a staple food during hot summer days as it is known to keep your body cool.

—It is mainly eaten with rice, and this is meant to be the first dish eaten during a meal, acting as a cleanser for your stomach.

—It is better for the curd to be fresh; it shouldn't be too sour or too bland.

—The seasoning and grated coconut can be avoided if you don't want to use too much *ghee* or coconut. If you use coconut then it should be freshly grated.

—Instead of tempering with *ghee*, you can also roast cumin seeds and curry leaves in a dry pan, grind in a mixer-grinder and use as seasoning.

Curd Curry

Lina Vincent

Serves 2–4

1 medium-sized onion
150 g potato
2 tsp oil
10 curry leaves
A pinch of turmeric powder
Salt to taste
3 cups curd

MASALA:
1 tsp cumin seeds
4–5 cloves of garlic
2-inch piece of ginger
2 green chillies

GARNISH:
1 tomato
1 sprig of coriander leaves

Finely chop garlic, ginger, and green chillies, and crush them with cumin seeds in a mortar and pestle until it becomes a coarse paste. Chop potato into medium-sized chunks and boil in water till it is almost cooked. Drain and keep aside. Finely chop the onion.

In a *kadhai,* heat 2 tsp of oil and add crushed spices. Stir for 2 to 4 minutes, till it turns aromatic. Add chopped onions and stir until they are pink and translucent. Add turmeric powder and curry leaves, and stir again. Next, add boiled potatoes and salt to taste, and stir over a medium flame for 5 minutes. Shift to low flame for 2 minutes and then add curd. Stir for another 1 to 2 minutes and turn off the stove.

Garnish with finely-chopped tomatoes and coriander leaves, and serve with hot rice.

Notes:
—Potatoes can be replaced with French beans, pumpkin, or other vegetables—except okra and brinjal.

—The consistency of the curd should be neither too thick nor too thin.

—To reduce spiciness use half the quantity of ginger and chilli or add more curd.

—Do not heat the curd. For reheating, place the dish in a bowl of hot water and stir gently.

—The recipe can be multiplied easily for larger servings.

—This curd preparation is a combination of what I learnt from my Mangalorean mother and my (late) Malayali mother-in-law. It is usually made as an accompaniment to other vegetarian or non-vegetarian dishes.

DIPS

Curd and Dill Dip ✦ Beetroot Dip ✦ Hummus ✦ Avocado and Raw Mango Dip ✦ Pomegranate Dip ✦ Curry Leaf Dip

Curd and Dill Dip

Suresh Jayaram

Serves 10

1 l curd
½ tsp ground black peppercorns
A small bunch of dill leaves
½ tsp salt

Hang curd in muslin cloth till the water drains completely. Squeeze out the remaining water. Shift the thick curd into a bowl and add ground peppercorns, salt, and finely-chopped dill leaves. Mix well.

Serve with crackers and chips, or as a spread with toast.

Notes:
—If you want the dip to be creamy add 2 tsp of cheese spread.

—Dill leaves can be substituted with chopped spring onions for a different flavour.

Beetroot Dip

Suresh Jayaram

Serves 10

4 beetroots
4 tomatoes
2 onions
10 cloves of garlic
4 tsp oil
Salt to taste

Peel beetroots, dice into cubes, boil, drain, and keep aside. Finely chop tomatoes, onions, and garlic, and fry them in a frying pan with oil. Continue frying until they turn brown. Add the boiled beetroot to the mixture in the pan and sauté for 2 minutes. Blend in a mixer-grinder with salt to taste.

Serve with crackers, chips, or baked *nippattu* (savoury cracker) from the local Iyengar bakery.

Notes:
—You can add about 3 to 4 dry red chillies to balance the sweetness.

—You could also stir the dip with some hung curd for variation. It turns dark pink in colour.

Hummus

Suresh Jayaram

Serves 10–15

500 g chickpeas
12 tsp olive oil
10 cloves of garlic
1 lime
Salt to taste

Soak chickpeas overnight. The next day, boil chickpeas in a pressure cooker with some salt till they turn mushy (four to five whistles). Once the pressure is released, remove and drain.

Peel and finely chop garlic. Fry them in a pan on low flame till they brown, with 2 tsp of olive oil. Blend chickpeas, garlic, and 10 tsp of olive oil in the mixer-grinder. Squeeze in a lime to make it tart.

Serve with crackers, cut carrots, cucumbers, or toast.

Notes:
—You can add a bit of chilli or black pepper powder on top to add some zing.

—You can also add 2 tbsp of tahini to give it a nutty flavour and texture.

Avocado and Raw Mango Dip

Suresh Jayaram

Serves 10

1 raw *thothapuri* mango
2 medium-sized ripe avocados
1 tsp red chilli powder
4 tsp olive oil
1 lime
Salt to taste

Scoop the flesh of the avocados from their skin and mash. Deseed the mango and dice into small pieces. Blend mango and avocado in a mixer-grinder, with olive oil, red chilli powder, and salt to taste. Empty into a bowl and squeeze in the juice of a lime before serving.

Serve with crackers or salted potato chips.

Notes:
—If *thothapuri* is not available, any other sour raw mango can be used as a substitute.

—Red chilli powder can be substituted with black pepper powder.

Pomegranate Dip

Smitha Cariappa

Serves 8–12

1 kg pomegranate
1 cup sugar
1 cup water
½ tsp cinnamon powder
1 tsp red chilli flakes
½ cup lime juice
½ cup finely-chopped dried orange preserved rinds

Finely chop orange rind and keep aside. Remove pomegranate kernels and boil in ½ cup of water until it reduces and thickens to ¼ of the original quantity. Allow it to cool. Then, blend it in a mixer-grinder for a few seconds. Remove from the mixer-grinder, add sugar and the remaining ½ cup of water to this, and boil again. Add lime juice, cinnamon powder, and chilli flakes and stir until it gets thick. Add dried orange rind and stir well.

Serve with *naan* or bread and preserve in an airtight bottle.

Curry Leaf Dip

Bharathesh GD

Serves 6

1 l curd
100 g of curry leaves
6–8 dried salty-curd chillies (*mor-milagai*)
½ bowl roasted peanuts
10 tbsp oil
2 tbsp olive oil
Salt to taste

Tie 1 litre of curd in a muslin cloth and hang for 2 to 3 hours.

Heat oil in a frying pan and fry salty-curd chillies till they turn golden-brown. Remove and deep-fry curry leaves in the same pan until they turn crisp. Roughly crush the leaves.

In a bowl, mix hung curd, fried curd chillies, and ¾ of the crushed curry leaves, along with salt to taste. Keep in mind that the fried chillies are salty too. Garnish with crushed roasted peanuts, the remaining curry leaves, and olive oil.

Serve with chips, nachos, bread, or cut salad vegetables.

Notes:
—This recipe can also be made with dill instead of curry leaves, and can be used as a spread for sandwiches.

CHUTNEYS

Sweet and Sour Mango Chutney ✦ Coconut Chutney ✦ Coconut Fried Gram Chutney ✦ Peanut Chutney ✦ Coco-mint Chutney ✦ Horse Gram Chutney ✦ Heerekai Chutney ✦ Raw Mango Chutney ✦ Gongura Chutney ✦ Thecha

Sweet and Sour Mango Chutney

Suresh Jayaram

Serves 6–8

2 half-ripe mangoes
A lime-sized ball of tamarind
4 dates
1 tsp red chilli powder
2 tsp oil
Salt to taste

Peel skin off mangoes, deseed, and dice into small cubes. Add diced mangoes, deseeded dates, red chilli powder, salt, and oil into a mixer-grinder and grind till smooth. Empty into a bowl.

Soak the ball of tamarind in hot water, until it is soft. Once it cools, squeeze out the pulp and pour into the ground mixture.

Mix well and serve with meals as a chutney, or with chips and crackers as a dip.

Notes:
—The dates in the recipe can be replaced with 2 tsp of jaggery powder.

Coconut Chutney

Dr. Hemalatha Bhuvanendra

Serves 6–8

½ cup grated coconut
4 green chillies
A handful of coriander leaves
½ tsp tamarind paste
¼ glass water
Salt to taste

TEMPERING:
1 tbsp oil
½ tsp mustard seeds
1 sprig of curry leaves

Grind grated coconut, green chillies, coriander leaves, tamarind paste, and salt in a mixer-grinder with ¼ glass of water.

Heat oil in a pan and add mustard seeds. Once they splutter, add curry leaves and turn off the flame. Use this as tempering for the chutney.

Serve with *dosa*, *idli*, and snacks.

Coconut Fried Gram Chutney

Dr. Hemalatha Bhuvanendra

Serves 4

100 g grated coconut
100 g fried gram *dal*
4 green chillies
A marble-sized ball of tamarind
10 coriander leaves
1 tsp oil
¼ glass water
A pinch of turmeric powder
Salt to taste

Chop green chillies and coriander leaves. Heat 1 tsp oil in a pan and fry green chillies for about a minute. Add tamarind, coriander leaves, and fried gram, and fry for another 1 to 2 minutes. Switch off the flame. In a mixer-grinder, grind this with grated coconut, turmeric powder, salt, and ¼ glass of water.

Serve with *dosa*, *idli*, and snacks.

Peanut Chutney

Dr. Hemalatha Bhuvanendra

Serves 4

125 g peanuts
4 green chillies
A handful of coriander leaves
½ tsp tamarind paste
1 clove of garlic
¼ glass water
Salt to taste

Chop green chillies, garlic, and coriander leaves, and keep aside. Roast peanuts in a pan until golden-brown and keep aside to cool. Grind chillies, garlic, coriander leaves, and fried peanuts in a mixer-grinder. To the ground chutney, add salt and tamarind paste, and blend well. After it is fully ground, add ¼ glass of water and blend once more while checking for consistency.

Serve with *dosa*, *idli*, and snacks.

Coco-mint Chutney

Maureen Gonsalves

Serves 6

1 cup fresh coconut
1 packed cup fresh mint leaves
¼ cup raisins
½ small onion
3–4 green chillies
3 cloves of garlic
½-inch piece of ginger
1 lime
1 tsp salt

Grate coconut and wash mint leaves thoroughly. Peel onion, garlic, and ginger. Extract juice from lime.

Place all ingredients mentioned above, along with raisins, green chillies, and salt, in a food processor (or mixer-grinder) and blend till smooth. Do not add any water. Taste and adjust seasoning.

Garnish with a sprig of mint leaves and serve as an accompaniment to any meal—as a versatile spread or a tangy dip. Great in sandwiches, on plain toast, or with cheese in toasted sandwiches.

Notes:
—Substitute raisins with 1 tsp of brown sugar or jaggery, if desired.

Horse Gram Chutney

Smitha Cariappa

Serves 4–6

3 tbsp horse gram
½ coconut
4 dry red chillies
A marble-sized ball of tamarind
Salt to taste

Grate coconut and deseed chillies. Dry roast horse gram. Mix all the ingredients in a mixer-grinder and grind to a smooth paste. Add a little water, if necessary, making sure the chutney's consistency stays thick.

Serve with *dosa*, *idli* and snacks.

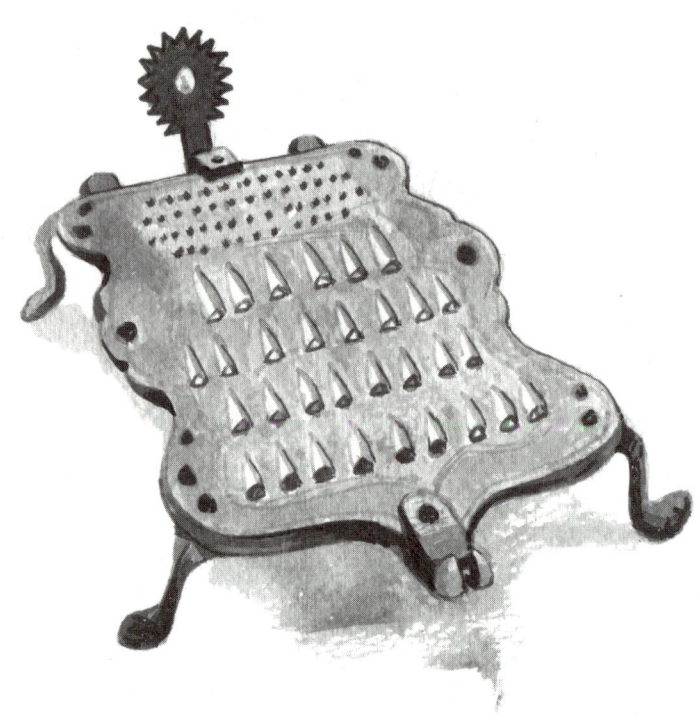

Heerekai Chutney

(Ridge Gourd Chutney)

Mohanavathi V

Serves 6–8

A handful of peanuts
2 tbsp *urad dal*
5 dry red chillies
4 cloves of garlic
1 ridge gourd
A marble-sized ball of tamarind
A handful of coriander leaves
Salt to taste

TEMPERING:
1 tsp mustard seeds
6–8 curry leaves
1 tsp oil

Chop and deseed ridge gourd. Chop coriander leaves. Keep aside.

In a *kadhai*, roast peanuts and *urad dal* till they turn brown. Add chillies and coriander leaves into the pan and fry till the coriander leaves wilt. Then add chopped ridge gourd, tamarind, garlic, and salt to taste. Fry till cooked. Once it is done, allow it to cool and then grind this mixture in a mixer-grinder.

In a separate frying pan, temper mustard seeds and curry leaves in 1 tsp of oil. Add this to the blended chutney and mix.

Serve with *dosa*, *idli*, and snacks.

Raw Mango Chutney

Mohanavathi V

Serves 6–8

2 raw mangoes
2 tbsp oil
2 tbsp *urad dal*
2 tbsp *chana dal*
4 dry red chillies
½ tsp fenugreek seeds
Salt to taste

TEMPERING:
1 tbsp oil
1 tsp mustard seeds
10 curry leaves
A pinch of asafoetida

Grate mangoes and keep aside. In a frying pan, heat 2 tbsp of oil. Add *urad dal, chana dal*, red chillies, and fenugreek seeds. Sauté lightly until they are roasted. Add grated mango to the frying pan and cook until the mixture obtains the consistency of a chutney. Add salt to taste.

In a separate smaller frying pan, temper mustard seeds and curry leaves in 1 tbsp of oil. Add a pinch of asafoetida powder. Once done, add this to the chutney and mix.

Serve with *dosa*, *idli*, and snacks.

Notes:
—The variety of mango you choose can be any sweet and sour mango, such as *thothapuri*.

Gongura Chutney
(Roselle Leaf Chutney)

Mohanavathi V

Serves 10–12

2 bunches of *gongura* leaves
10–15 green chillies
Salt to taste
3 bulbs of garlic
2 tbsp fenugreek seeds
1 tbsp mustard seeds
10 curry leaves
A pinch of asafoetida
15 tbsp sesame oil

Finely chop green chillies. Wash and separate leaves of the *gongura* from the stem. Keep aside.

Take 5 tbsp of oil in a pan and fry green chillies. Once fried, remove the green chillies leaving behind the oil. In the same pan, add *gongura* leaves in small batches, frying them till they shrivel and turn completely brown. Add salt to taste while frying. Once all the *gongura* leaves are fried, keep them aside and let them cool. After cooling, grind *gongura* leaves and green chillies together in the mixer grinder.

Peel garlic cloves and crush them in a mortar and pestle. Dry roast fenugreek seeds, let it cool, and powder it coarsely in a mortar and pestle (or mixer-grinder).

Heat 10 tbsp of oil in the pan, add in mustard seeds, curry leaves, crushed garlic, fenugreek powder, and a pinch of asafoetida. Once this is roasted, add in ground *gongura* and chillies, and mix well.

Serve as a pickle with meals or as a chutney with *dosa* and *idli*. Traditionally it is mixed in cooked rice with sesame or groundnut oil and eaten as a dish in itself.

Notes:
—Sometimes while frying the *gongura* leaves, they may become slimy. This is natural and will disappear as you continue to cook it.

Thecha

Rucha Vibhute

Serves 6–8

20–25 green chillies
15–20 cloves of garlic
1 sprig of coriander leaves
1 tsp cumin seeds
2½ tbsp peanuts
3 tsp peanut oil
Coarse sea salt to taste

Heat oil in a pan, and sauté chillies and garlic on high flame. Be careful as the chillies can pop. Add cumin seeds, coriander leaves with the stem, and peanuts. Remove from flame, cool, and pound all the ingredients, along with salt, in a mortar and pestle until everything comes together.

Serve with wheat *chapati, jowar, baajra,* or rice flour *bhakri* and sliced onion, curd, and chutney.

Notes:
—Peanuts are optional.

—Peanut oil can be replaced with any vegetable or sunflower oil.

—A popular variation is with *amsool*— dry kokum fruit.

—*Thecha* is a staple diet of the agricultural community in Maharashtra, Gujarat, Rajasthan, and some parts of Karnataka.

PICKLES AND RELISHES

Nelikkai Thokku ✦ Chintakaya Thokku ✦ Prawn Dosakaya Pickle ✦ Raw Mango Pickle ✦ Raw Black Pepper Pickle ✦ Jajju Mullangi ✦ Puliyodharai Mix ✦ Puli Inji ✦ Sumana's Gokarna Heerekai Gojju ✦ Tomato Gojju ✦ Banana Rasayana ✦ Chilli Peanut Butter

Nelikkai Thokku

(Indian Gooseberry Thokku)

Suresh Jayaram

Makes 500 g

500 g *amla* (Indian gooseberry)
10 green chillies
A pinch of asafoetida
10 tbsp oil
Salt to taste

MASALA:
1 tbsp mustard seeds
½ tbsp cumin seeds
1 tbsp fenugreek seeds

Pressure cook *amla* in water till it is soft and falls off the seed. Deseed and keep aside. Slit green chillies lengthwise and keep aside.

Roast mustard seeds, cumin seeds, and fenugreek seeds, and let it cool. Grind them together coarsely.

Heat 10 tbsp of oil in a saucepan. Add green chillies and fry on a low flame till they change colour. Add the freshly ground *masala* and asafoetida, and let it cook in the oil for a few minutes. Add deseeded *amla* and stir well. Add salt to taste and let it cool. Once this cools, coarsely blend in a mixer-grinder.

Store refrigerated in an air-tight bottle.

Notes:
—Only use a dry spoon while serving because there is very little oil as preservative.

Chintakaya Thokku

(Raw Tamarind Thokku)

Raghu Tenkayala

Makes 250 g

100 g raw tamarind
1 tsp turmeric powder
Rock salt to taste
A handful of roasted peanuts
2 green chillies
A few sprigs of coriander leaves
4–5 cloves of garlic
1 cucumber

TEMPERING:
2 tbsp oil
½ tsp *chana dal*
½ tsp *urad dal*
½ tsp cumin seeds
½ tsp mustard seeds
3 dry red chillies
10 curry leaves

Grind raw tamarind, turmeric powder, and rock salt into a coarse paste. Separately grind roasted peanuts, green chillies, coriander leaves, and garlic cloves into a coarse paste. Mix both and keep aside. Finely dice cucumber and keep aside.

Heat 2 tbsp of oil in a pan and add *chana dal*, *urad dal*, cumin seeds, mustard seeds, red chillies broken in half, and curry leaves. Once the mustard seeds splutter, add in the mixed paste and finely-diced cucumber. Cook on medium flame for a few minutes.

Store refrigerated in an air-tight bottle.

Notes:
—Usually the paste of raw green tamarind, turmeric powder, and rock salt is readily available in Telugu neighbourhoods such as VV Puram in Bangalore or can be bought from most regions in Andhra Pradesh, Telangana, or Bellary. This preserve forms the base for various chutneys.

Prawn Dosakaya Pickle

(Prawn Mangalore Cucumber Pickle)

Amshu Chukki

Makes 500 g

1 *dosakaya*
350 g small prawns
6 cloves of garlic
½ cup mustard seeds
6–7 fenugreek seeds
½ cup red chilli powder
½ cup salt
1 cup sesame or vegetable oil
½ lime

Deseed the cucumber, cut into ¼-inch cubes, and keep aside in a bowl. Deep-fry prawns till they are nearly golden-brown. Remove from pan and keep aside. In the same oil, fry cloves of garlic, remove, and let the oil cool.

Add ½ tsp of salt into the bowl of cucumber pieces and let it rest for about 15 minutes. Then, squeeze and drain water from the cucumber pieces.

Grind mustard seeds and fenugreek seeds into a coarse powder. Take a large dry bowl and mix the ground powder along with chilli powder. To this, add ¼ cup of salt, leaving the rest to be added later if needed. In another bowl, mix cucumber pieces with prawns and pour ½ a cup of the cooled oil into this. Coat all the pieces evenly. Now, begin gradually adding the powder mixture from the first bowl into the second bowl while stirring constantly, making sure no lumps are formed. Once mixed, add garlic, squeeze in the lime, and pour in the remaining ½ cup of oil. Mix well and let it rest overnight. Taste the next day and add salt if needed.

Shift into a glass bottle and store refrigerated.

Raw Mango Pickle

Dr. Lakshmi Devi

Makes 500 g

1 kg raw mango
30 g salt
2 tsp red chilli powder
2 tsp fenugreek seeds
2 tsp sesame seeds
1 tsp black peppercorns
1 tsp cumin seeds
½ tsp onion seeds
1 tsp turmeric powder
10 cloves of garlic
10 cloves
5 small cinnamon sticks
100 g jaggery powder
100 ml vinegar
1 cup oil

Peel and grate mangoes. Add all the ingredients to the grated mangoes (except the vinegar) and mix in a jar. Place the jar in the sun for a day. Next day, add the vinegar, so that it covers the contents of the jar. Let it mature for 10 to 15 days and then consume.

Store refrigerated in an air-tight bottle.

Raw Black Pepper Pickle

Sarasija Subramanian

Makes 500 g

200 g raw black pepper stalks
1 raw mango
2-inch piece of ginger
4 limes
3 tbsp salt
500 ml water

Chop the raw mango into thin 2-inch pieces and dice the ginger. Cut the limes in half, squeeze out the juice, and keep aside. Remove seeds and finely dice the lime peels.

In a small pot, boil 100 ml water with 3 tbsp of salt till it dissolves. Pour this into a jar with the other 400 ml of water. Add raw mango, ginger, lime juice, and lime peels, along with raw black pepper stalks.

Close the jar tightly and let the pickle soak for at least 1 week before serving.

Notes:
—The pepper should be tender. If it begins to dry then it wont soak-in the brine.

—The pickle must be refrigerated and the lime juice should not be scrimped on as that is the only preservative along with salt.

—Ensure that the green pepper stalks are always submerged in brine or they will begin to blacken and dry.

Jajju Mullangi
(Mashed Radish Relish)

Basavachar S

Serves 4

3 radishes
A lime-sized ball of tamarind
½ tbsp crushed black peppercorns
3–4 green chillies
2 onions
½ cup water
Salt to taste

Peel and pound radishes. Finely chop green chillies and onions. Soak all the listed ingredients in ½ a cup of water for at least an hour.

Serve as a side dish or pickle.

Notes:
—The longer you allow the ingredients to soak, the more the radish will take in the flavour of the tamarind, making it a lot stronger—like a pickle.

Puliyodharai Mix

Mariraj Rajasekaran

Serves 4

A big-tomato-sized ball of tamarind
25 dry red chillies
1 tsp fenugreek seeds
1 tsp *urad dal*
2 tsp black sesame seeds
2 tbsp fried peanuts
2 bunches of curry leaves
1 tbsp *chana dal*
½ tsp asafoetida
½ tsp turmeric powder
5 tbsp sesame oil
Salt to taste
1 tsp jaggery

Soak tamarind in hot water for 10 minutes. Extract its juice and keep aside. Roast 20 red chillies in a pan without oil, making sure to remove them before they blacken, and keep aside. Roast fenugreek seeds and once they turn light brown, remove from the flame. Powder the fenugreek seeds and red chillies with asafoetida powder in a mixer-grinder. Separately roast black sesame seeds and *urad dal*, without oil, and powder together. Keep both powders aside.

In a pan, add 3 tbsp sesame oil and fry *chana dal*. Add peanuts, 5 red chillies, and curry leaves. After a minute, add in the extracted tamarind juice, salt, and turmeric powder. Once the tamarind juice starts to boil, cover the pan, and leave for about 10 minutes on a low flame. Then, add the first powder (with fenugreek seeds) and let it boil on a low flame until the oil gets separated and floats on top. This should take about 5 to 10 minutes. Finally add the second powder, jaggery, and the remaining 2 tbsp of oil and remove from flame.

Add this preparation to cooked rice to make *puliyodharai* or serve with *idli*, *dosa*, or *upma*.

Notes:
—This *puliyodharai* recipe is in my native Thanjavur Pillai style. It can be stored outside the refrigerator for about a week without spoiling as it is fully submerged in oil.

Puli Inji

(Tamarind Ginger Relish)

Kadamboor Neeraj

Serves 4

2 green chillies
1 cup jaggery powder
1 tsp salt
200 g ginger
250 g dried tamarind
500 ml water

TEMPERING:
2 tsp mustard seeds
1 dry red chilli
6–10 curry leaves
4 tbsp coconut or gingelly oil

Slit green chillies lengthwise; peel and grate ginger. Soak dried tamarind in about 500 ml of hot (but not boiling) water, and set aside. Once it has softened completely, squeeze and sieve the pulp. In a pot, heat the sieved liquid on a slow flame. Once it begins to simmer, add ginger and green chillies. As it nears boiling, add jaggery. Once the jaggery has completely dissolved, add salt. Let it cook on a low flame for about 10 minutes. The mixture should be fairly viscous and not runny.

In a separate *kadhai*, heat oil and temper mustard seeds, dry red chilli, and curry leaves. When done, pour into the cooked *puli inji* and set aside for a while.

Serve like a pickle or alternatively as a dip or chutney. It can be served chilled as well and stored refrigerated for a few weeks.

Notes:
—While tempering, you can add fenugreek seeds with the mustard seeds.

—The ratio of tamarind, ginger, and jaggery can be altered to suit personal tastes.

Sumana's Gokarna Heerekai Gojju

(Sumana's Gokarna Ridge Gourd Gojju)

Arunesh Maiyer

Serves 6

400 g ridge gourd
1 cup grated coconut
1 tbsp tamarind paste
2 heaped tbsp chopped coriander leaves
Salt to taste
1½ cups water

MASALA:
1 flat tbsp *urad dal*
2 pinches of mustard seeds
6–8 Byadagi chillies

TEMPERING:
1 tbsp coconut oil
½ tsp mustard seeds
1 flat tsp *urad dal*
4 pinches of turmeric powder
⅛ tsp asafoetida
2 whole Byadagi chillies
8 fresh curry leaves

Finely chop coriander leaves. Peel ridge gourd ensuring that the hard ridge and green skin is removed clean. Dice them 1 cm long and pressure cook with 1½ cups of water, allowing for two whistles. When the steam has escaped, remove the ridge gourd from the cooker. Drain the leftover water into a bowl and keep it aside till it reaches room temperature; spread boiled gourd on a plate to cool completely. You can refrigerate it to expedite the cooling.

In a tempering spoon, take less than ½ a tsp of coconut oil and add 1 tsp of *urad dal* till it turns a deep golden-brown. When you get a woody smoky smell, gently remove only the *urad dal* and keep aside, retaining the little oil in the tempering spoon. Next take 2 pinches of mustard seeds and fry in the same oil. This will take a few seconds. Remove the seeds from the spoon and keep aside separately. Remember not to mix it with the *urad dal*. Add a few drops of coconut oil into the tempering spoon (only if no oil is remaining) and fry red chillies broken into 1-inch pieces. Once fried, remove from flame and add to the mustard seeds. Allow it to cool.

In a mixer-grinder put the freshly grated coconut, tempered mustard seeds, Byadagi chillies, and tamarind paste, and grind. The coconut must be pulverised to the texture of a fine powder. Now add salt accordingly. At this point, add just enough of the cooled cooking water into the blender to get a saucy texture which is not too runny or firm. Now add the cooled ridge gourd and briefly pulse the blender once or twice for a few seconds. The idea is to get a taste of ridge gourd, with no chunks. Now add fried *urad dal* and blend it briskly to a coarse consistency. This will give off a faint roasted *urad* flavour. Taste to check for salt and tamarind balance. Pour into a serving bowl, ensuring that the texture is that of a saucy fluid. Sprinkle chopped coriander and stir.

In a tempering spoon, heat 1 tbsp of coconut oil and start introducing each ingredient, one by one in the given order. Mustard seeds go in first; wait till they crackle and follow it with *urad dal*, turmeric powder, and whole red chillies. Then add asafoetida and lastly curry leaves. Stir all ingredients lightly till the curry leaves turn crisp and mix into the bowl with the paste.

Serve at room temperature or slightly cool (after a brief refrigeration), with fluffy rice, *roti, poori, dosa*, or even hot linguine or spaghetti.

Notes:
—A brief note on *gojjus*: *gojju* means different things in various regions of Karnataka, but in Gokarna cuisine it is a not-so-runny sauce, served with fluffy steamed rice. Visualise a slightly runny chutney and you will get the picture.

—The ridge gourd should be firm. Ensure that the ridges have not turned brown.

—If you are using pre-grated coconut from a packet (the readymade stuff), keep it out of the refrigerator for a while and allow it to thaw.

—The *urad dal* used for this recipe should be split and de-skinned.

—If possible, obtain Byadagi chillies from Haveri district for this recipe. This is the preferred choice.

—The *bagaar* or tempering is called *vaggarnay* in Kannada.

—Each spice should be fried one at a time till you fathom different heating levels of each spice and can figure how to add them one after the other into the same tempering spoon. This comes with practice.

—Any flavour-free vegetable oil can be used as a substitute for coconut oil.

Tomato Gojju

Basavachar S

Serves 4

500 g tomatoes
3 onions
15 cloves of garlic
½ tsp jaggery powder
1-inch piece of ginger
Salt to taste
A pinch of asafoetida
1 tbsp mustard seeds
1 tbsp cumin seeds
3 sprigs of curry leaves
4 green chillies
1 tbsp *ghee*
4 tbsp groundnut oil

GARNISH:
1 sprig of coriander leaves

Crush cloves of garlic and finely chop onions, ginger, green chillies, and tomatoes.

Heat oil and *ghee* in a pan and add mustard seeds. Once they splutter, add cumin seeds, curry leaves, and asafoetida. Add crushed garlic, onions, and green chillies with a little salt. Once the onions turn reddish-brown, add tomatoes. Cook till the tomatoes begin to sweat and add salt to taste. Once half-cooked, add jaggery powder and continue to cook the mixture till it thickens.

Garnish with chopped coriander leaves and serve as a side dish with *dosa, idli, akki rotti, chapati,* or rice.

Banana Rasayana
(Banana Relish)

NS Harsha

Serves 2

1 large ripe banana
½ tbsp sugar (brown or white)
1 tbsp grated coconut
2 pods of green cardamom

Cut banana into medium thin slices. Transfer the cut pieces into a bowl and add grated coconut, sugar, and 2 ground green cardamom. Mix well and leave it (in the refrigerator or outside) for 5 to 6 minutes while the sugar melts completely.

It is ready to serve!

Notes:
—You can replace sugar with honey.

—This recipe has been previously published in the Artists Cookbook by Mori Art Museum (MAM) in 2020.

—The recipe is in collaboration with my mother—Chandrika MN.

Chilli Peanut Butter

Biju Cherayath

Makes 1½ kg

1 kg peanuts
12 Byadagi chillies
300 g sugar
1 tbsp groundnut oil
A pinch of salt

Slow roast peanuts in an iron wok with a pinch of salt and 1 tbsp of groundnut oil. Remove skin and keep aside.

Take the dry grinder jar of the mixer-grinder and grind ¼ of the peanuts. If it gets stuck, add a few drops of groundnut oil. Slowly you will find the oil from the peanuts will start coming out and make a smooth paste. Grind the remaining peanuts and other ingredients. Make sure all the ingredients are well mixed finally to make a homogeneous mixture. All ingredients can be adjusted to suit your palate. Do remember to add a pinch of salt in the end.

Serve with bread or toast.

Notes:
—Sugar can be replaced with jaggery powder.

—If your jar is not large enough to hold all the ingredients then grind little by little.

SWEETS AND DESSERTS

Kajjaaya ✦ Hollige ✦ Peanut Coconut Barfi ✦ Bamboo Rice Payasam ✦ Koovale Puttu ✦ Fruit Custard ✦ Tender Coconut Pudding ✦ Chocolate Olive Oil Cake ✦ Gluten-free Chocolate Cake with Almond Flour ✦ Orange Cardamom Cake ✦ Citrus Semolina Cake ✦ Cooker Cake ✦ Fudgy Brownies ✦ Coffee Cake ✦ Rich Christmas Fruit Cake ✦ Black Forest Cookies ✦ Peanut Butter Blossom Cookies

Kajjaaya

Dr. Hemalatha Bhuvanendra

Makes 15–20 kajjaayas

250 g red rice flour
250 g jaggery
25 g sesame seeds
5–6 pods of green cardamom
1 small glass water
Oil for frying

Heat a thick-bottomed pot over a low flame. Add a small glass of water with jaggery and keep stirring till jaggery melts. Test the consistency by putting a drop in a bowl of water; if it is sticky and yet holds its shape, it is ready. Add red rice flour, spoon by spoon, into the liquid on the stove and keep stirring till its consistency becomes semi-solid. Add sesame seeds and crushed cardamom, and stir well. Keep aside to cool for 5 to 6 hours.

Make lime-sized balls out of this semi-solid mixture and flatten them in your palm. Fry them in a pan of hot oil on a low flame until they become golden-brown on both sides.

Serve warm.

Notes:
—To make red rice flour, take red rice and soak it in water for 5 to 6 hours. Drain and dry in shade. Once dry, grind to a fine powder in a mixer grinder.

Hollige

Dr. Hemalatha Bhuvanendra

Makes 10–12 holliges

DOUGH:
125 g semolina
125 g refined wheat flour
½ tsp turmeric powder
250–300 ml oil
¼ glass water

FILLING:
250 g *toor dal*
125 g jaggery
A handful of grated coconut
6 pods of green cardamom
Water as required

For the dough, mix semolina and wheat flour with some turmeric powder, 1 tsp of oil, and ¼ glass of water. Knead into a ball of dough and pour enough oil to completely cover the dough; soak overnight.

For the filling, boil *toor dal* in water in a 1:1 ratio. When fully cooked, grind into a fine paste with jaggery, grated coconut, and cardamom seeds (without the peel) in a mixer-grinder. Make golf-ball-sized balls from this paste and keep aside.

Take a sheet of aluminium foil and smear oil on it. Place a lime-sized portion of the dough and flatten it with your hands till it becomes a flat disc. Make sure to keep dipping your hand in oil ever so often so that it doesn't become dry. Then, place the filling in the centre of this disc and fold it in to make a ball. Once again smear oil on the foil, dip your hand in oil, and flatten the ball with your hand to make it into a thin disc. Fry this on a *tawa* with oil over a slow flame. Repeat the steps for the remaining pieces.

Serve with *ghee* or milk.

Notes:
—This dish is commonly referred to as *obbattu* and is made for Varalaxmi Puja and Ugadi.

Peanut Coconut Barfi

Shanthi Kasi

Makes 20–25 barfis

500 g peanuts
100 g grated desiccated coconut
250 g sugar
¾–1 cup water
Ghee as needed

Roast peanuts in a heavy-bottomed pan for 10 to 15 minutes. Remove from flame and cool. Remove skin from peanuts and grind coarsely in a mixer-grinder. Mix this with desiccated coconut and keep aside.

Heat ¾ cup of water in a pan. When hot, add sugar and stir until it dissolves. Let the syrup boil for some time. Take a drop of the syrup and place it in a small cup of water. If you are able to roll it into a ball the syrup is ready. Switch off the flame and add the coconut and peanut mixture. Mix well.

Pour this mixture into a deep plate greased with *ghee* and pat it down to a ¾-inch thick layer. When half-cooled, cut into rectangles or squares. Once completely cool, remove the individual pieces carefully from the plate.

Serve as dessert or alternatively as a snack.

Notes:
—Cut into the *barfi* when it is semi-cooled as this won't be possible when the mixture cools completely since it hardens.

—The key lies in making the syrup right. It may take a few tries. If the syrup is underdone, the *barfi* won't set. However, in this case, you can roll the mixture into small balls. If the syrup gets overdone, the mixture will get flaky. Just enjoy the flakiness. The combination of sugar, peanut, and coconut is edible any which way and your effort won't be wasted.

—The word *'barfi'* or *'burfi'* originated from the Persian word *'barf'* or *'burf'* which means 'a slab of ice'. *Barfi* looks like an ice cube. It is a high energy sweet and is made during festivals. It can also be consumed during fasts.

—Being healthy and nutritious, in its modern avatar, the *barfi* is known as an 'energy bar'. It also qualifies as a vegan dessert.

—Some temples serve these ingredients as *prasad* in a raw form—a mix of coconut, peanut, and sugar.

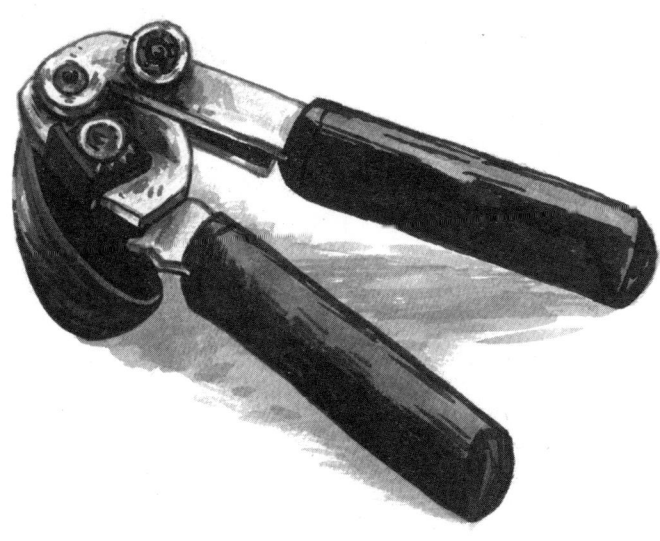

Bamboo Rice Payasam

Sitikanta Samantsinghar

Serves 6–8

1 cup condensed milk
¼ tsp cardamom powder
1 cup bamboo rice
4 cups full cream milk (or plant-based milk)
1 tbsp *ghee*
8–10 cashew nuts
A handful of raisins

Wash and soak bamboo rice in water for 3 to 4 hours. Drain water and pressure cook the rice in 3 cups of milk for three whistles. Meanwhile, take *ghee* in a small pan and fry cashew nuts till golden-brown; then fry raisins.

Open the lid of the pressure cooker (careful while letting out the steam) and check the rice—it should be tender to touch. Add one more cup of milk and cook on medium flame. Keep stirring. When the preparation becomes really soft, add cardamom powder. Mix well. Add ½ a cup of condensed milk and check the sweetness. Once the condensed milk is added, do not allow it to boil as the milk tends to curdle. Continue to add more according to the level of sweetness desired. When achieved, bring it down to a simmer and remove from heat. Garnish with cashews and raisins fried in *ghee*, and mix well.

Serve hot.

Notes:
—Condensed milk can be replaced with jaggery syrup.

—Bamboo rice is the seed of a dying bamboo shoot, produced at the end of its life span. The reason this rice is uncommon is that it takes many years for an aged bamboo plant to flower.

—This recipe was made as a part of my project exhibited at the Open Studio of the Next-Step Residency 2018 in 1Shanthiroad.

Koovale Puttu

Renu Appachu

Makes 20 dumplings

500 g ripe jackfruit
½ cup jaggery powder
2 cups rice *rava*
5 pods of green cardamom
½ cup grated desiccated coconut
2 banana leaves
Water as required

Boil jaggery powder in water to make syrup. Strain and keep aside. Deseed jackfruit and grind its flesh into a pulp in the mixer-grinder. Mix jackfruit pulp, jaggery syrup, and rice *rava*. Add in crushed cardamom and desiccated coconut.

Make small golf-ball-sized balls and cut banana leaves into pieces large enough to cover them. Fold the dumplings into the banana leaf pieces and pin the edges with a toothpick. Steam for 10 minutes on a plate in a *kadhai* or on an *idli* plate.

After steaming, unpack the leaves and serve hot with *ghee*.

Fruit Custard

Suresh Jayaram

Serves 8–10

1 l milk
2 tsp custard powder
1 cup water
6 ripe bananas
2 apples
A handful of green grapes

OPTIONAL:
500 g tea cake from the local bakery

Chop bananas, dice apples, and deseed grapes.

Boil milk on a low flame. While the milk boils, add custard powder and water in a bowl and mix until it becomes a creamy sauce (making sure no lumps are formed). Add this creamy sauce into the boiling milk and stir vigorously so that the bottom of the pot doesn't burn the custard. The custard will start setting in approximately 5 minutes. Once set, switch off the flame and let it cool to room temperature. Then refrigerate until cold.

Add cut fruits to this custard before serving. Alternatively, line slices of tea cake in a serving dish and pour the chilled fruit custard over it.

Tender Coconut Pudding

Suresh Jayaram

Serves 8

1 l milk
1 tin condensed milk (400 g)
4 tender coconuts
4 tsp china grass powder (*agar agar*)

Scoop and thinly chop the flesh from tender coconuts, and keep aside. Bring milk to a boil and add china grass into it. Stir well, making sure it isn't lumpy. Add in condensed milk and thinly-chopped tender coconut. Stir well and once it thickens, remove from flame, cool, and refrigerate for an hour. Then, take it out and check for consistency—it should have become thick enough to cut into cubes.

Slice into large cubes and serve cold.

Chocolate Olive Oil Cake

Ashok Vish

Serves 6

125 ml water
50 g cocoa powder
125 g all-purpose flour
½ tsp baking soda
A pinch of salt
175 g powdered sugar
150 ml olive oil
3 eggs
2 tsp vanilla essence
A spoonful of butter

Preheat the oven to 170 degrees Celsius. Grease a cake tin with butter and sprinkle a pinch of flour. Boil 125 ml of water; remove from flame and add vanilla essence and cocoa powder. Whisk until smooth.

In a bowl, take flour, baking soda, and a pinch of salt. In another bowl, mix sugar and olive oil, and break eggs into it. Whisk this mixture for 3 minutes till a primrose color is reached. Pour the heated chocolate mixture into the primrose mixture and whisk until it merges well.

Sift the flour mixture and add it to the already combined mixture; stir with a spatula until there are no lumps. Pour this into the cake tin and bake in the preheated oven for 40 minutes.

Let it cool slightly and serve with whipped cream.

Notes:
— The difference between baking and cooking is that with baking there must be precision, no *andaaz* can be used.

—Avoid making the water and cocoa mixture into a thick paste, instead let it be runny. It tastes better that way.

—Use vanilla essence and not extract, since the essence is milder and will not overpower the taste of the cake.

—The flour can be substituted with ground almonds. Flour is the cheaper option and ground almonds is the healthier one.

Gluten-free Chocolate Cake with Almond Flour

Ayisha Abraham

Serves 4

170 g butter
170 g dark cooking chocolate
¼ cup sugar
2 eggs
¾ cup almond flour
1 tsp baking powder
¼ cup milk/cream
2 tsp vanilla essence
1 tbsp alcohol of your choice (rum, vodka, or brandy)

Melt chocolate, butter, and sugar together in a pan and cool it down.

In a blender, add almond flour, baking powder, eggs, milk or cream, vanilla essence, and 1 tbsp alcohol of your choice. Add molten chocolate, butter, and sugar and blend till smooth.

Bake in a preheated oven at 180 to 200 degrees Celsius for roughly 1 hour till firm but not dry. The consistency should be moist and gooey.

Serve warm.

Notes:
—I use Morde dark chocolate which is easily available—not chocolate compound—and fresh vanilla pods from Coorg soaked in vodka.

—This recipe is a recent version of a gluten-free cake that has, for me, become a signature recipe; a balm for stressful days. After all, there has to be something delicious and sinful that constitutes one's everyday—the gooey, dense, dark chocolate cake that also invites many variations.

—If almonds are too expensive and indulgent then it can be left out.

—Flavours can be added to it—mint or red chilli or orange rind—and it is like that panacea for when one has a craving post-dinner for something *meetha*.

Orange Cardamom Cake

Ashok Vish

Serves 6

130 g unsalted butter
150 g powdered sugar
Zest of 2 oranges
½ tsp vanilla extract
2 eggs
175 g all-purpose flour
50 g semolina
150 g sour cream or greek yogurt
12–15 pods of green cardamom
1 tsp ground cinnamon sticks
1½ tsp baking powder
½ tsp salt

ORANGE CARDAMOM SYRUP:
1 orange
½ lime
40 g powdered sugar
6 pods of green cardamom
30 ml citrus liqueur (eg. Cointreau, limoncello)

Preheat the oven to 170 degrees Celsius. Line a springform cake tin (or any circular cake pan) with baking paper or grease the sides using non-stick spray or even just butter.

In a large mixing bowl, soften butter, then mix it with sugar. Beat this together until pale and creamy. Beat in orange zest and vanilla extract. Add eggs, one after the other, beating well after each addition. Scrape down the sides of the bowl occasionally. Add crushed cardamom, cinnamon, baking powder, and salt. Gently mix in flour, semolina, and sour cream or greek yogurt. The batter must be quite thick. Pour the batter into the cake tin. Spread evenly and smoothen the top. Check that the oven has reached the correct temperature, then place the tin on the middle rack of the oven. Bake for 50 to 60 minutes. The cake is ready when golden-brown on top and a skewer into the centre comes out clean.

While it is baking, prepare the syrup. For this, juice the orange and lime into a saucepan. Add sugar, pods of cardamom, and liqueur. Heat the syrup gently over low heat, stirring until the sugar has dissolved. Let the syrup simmer for 5 minutes over low heat. Strain the syrup into a bowl and set aside.

When the cake is removed from the oven, poke about 50 holes all over the cake while it's still warm. Pour the syrup evenly over the cake. It looks like a lot of syrup, but the cake will soak it all up. Let the cake cool in the tin before releasing the clip.

Serve warm.

Notes:
—The citrus liqueur is optional.

Citrus Semolina Cake

Janet Burchill & Jennifer McCamley

Serves 10

125 g unsalted butter
1 tbsp finely-grated orange and lemon rind
1 cup caster sugar
2 eggs
⅔ cup semolina
1 ½ cups self-raising flour
½ cup milk

CITRUS SYRUP:
1 cup brown sugar
1 cup unstrained orange juice
1 small lemon
½ cup cold water

Preheat the oven to 180 degrees Celsius. Grease a 20-cm round springform cake tin. Line the base and sides with baking paper. Thinly slice a lemon and keep aside.

Using a hand mixer, beat softened butter with caster sugar, orange and lemon rind until pale and creamy. Beat in eggs. Stir in flour, semolina, and milk. Spread the mixture into the cake tin. Bake for 45 to 50 minutes.

For the citrus syrup, heat orange juice, sugar, and ½ cup of cold water in a saucepan over a low flame. When the sugar has dissolved, add lemon slices and increase heat to high. Boil without stirring for 5 minutes.

Pour half the syrup over the cake while warm. Turn out the cake onto a plate and arrange lemon slices on the top.

Serve with the remaining syrup drizzled over or on the side. Depending on preference, add cream or yoghurt.

Notes:
—We have been living in a region called Sunraysia since September 2019 and our house faces an orange grove. The choice of the cake recipe relates to us being here at the moment.

Cooker Cake

Yugashri Anandappa

Serves 6

2 cups *ragi* flour
4 tsp cocoa powder
2 tsp baking powder
2 bananas
1¼ cup sugar
4 eggs
1¼ cup oil
2 tsp orange/vanilla/pineapple essence
A fistful of dry fruits and nuts (raisins, almonds, cashews, walnuts)
Milk as needed

Sieve *ragi* flour, baking powder, and cocoa powder onto a newspaper and mix well. Keep aside. Blend bananas in a mixer-grinder. Break eggs into a small bowl and whisk for 2 to 3 minutes till a lather forms. Add sugar to this bowl and whisk further. Add oil and whisk again for 2 to 3 minutes. Add in the preferred essence and ground bananas, and whisk for an additional minute.

Add the sieved *ragi* flour, baking powder, and cocoa powder to this mixture and mix using your hands for some time, before using a whisk. Add a little milk and whisk if the mixture appears to be too dry. Finally, add a fistful of dry fruits and nuts of your choice and whisk.

Preheat a pressure cooker for 5 minutes on full flame. Pour the batter into a cake dish or mould and place into the cooker on a 1-inch raised stand. Close lid, without weight and gasket. Cook at full flame for 5 to 7 minutes, then on a low flame for 40 minutes. Open the lid and pierce a knife through the centre—if the knife comes out clean, the cake is cooked.

Serve while warm.

Notes:
—This batter has to be baked immediately, since storing it for more than 30 minutes will make it ferment.

—An aluminium cooker is preferred since the heat spreads more evenly as opposed to a steel cooker.

—If the batter turns out to be hard because of the cold weather, one can add more oil or milk.

—The mixture is sieved in the beginning, not to separate lumps as much as to mix the ingredients well.

—After the cake is done, take it out of the cooker and cover with a cotton cloth so that it retains its moisture and the crust doesn't harden.

—Dry fruits and nuts can be replaced with pumpkin seeds.

Fudgy Brownies

Manasa Kashi

Makes 10–12 pieces

150 g milk/dark cooking chocolate
100 g unsalted butter
¼ cup cocoa powder
175 g granulated sugar
2 tbsp milk
1 tsp vanilla essence
3 eggs
100 g all-purpose flour
½ tsp salt

Grease a 9-inch tin with butter and preheat the oven to 200 degrees Celsius. Chop cooking chocolate and melt it together with butter. This can be done in a bowl over boiling water or in the microwave in 10 to 20 second increments.

Whisk in cocoa powder, sugar, and vanilla essence. After making sure the mixture is no longer noticeably warm, add in eggs one by one. The temperature is really important here, because if the chocolate is still hot from melting, the eggs will cook and crystallise. Fold in flour and salt. While this recipe doesn't require sieving in flour, for the sake of incorporating air, it is worth it to take the time to ensure an even distribution of salt through the batter. Add in milk and pour into the greased tin, leveling out as far as possible. Feel free to tap the tin against the counter a few times; no need to worry about losing air.

Pop this into the oven, turning down the temperature to 180 degrees Celsius as you do. Bake for 20 to 25 minutes or until a toothpick comes out with 2 to 3 crumbs and no liquid.

Serve warm or cold. It is excellent with ice-cream.

Notes:
—You can use brown sugar here if you'd like a nuttier taste, but go with a full 200 g instead of just 175 g to preserve that level of sweetness.

—You can substitute all-purpose flour with whole wheat flour for a denser, fudgier brownie. Use 100 g, but add in 2 tbsp more milk because it tends to dry out otherwise.

—This brownie is quite fudgy by definition and it tends to catch on the bottom. It might be worth taking the time to line the bottom of the tin or, at the very least, coating it with flour after it's been greased with butter.

—If you want a crispy top, I would suggest keeping on the top coil in the oven for about 5 minutes of the baking time and then switching to bottom only.

—Even if you mess up and the egg cooks when adding into the butter-cocoa mixture, all is not lost. You can fix it by whisking in hot water 1 tsp at a time until it un-solidifies a little more. The final brownie will be a little more grainy than it would have been otherwise, but it is still salvageable.

—Most recipes will say to bake until a skewer comes out clean but this is a brownie, so it's going to be a little more wet. Additionally, it will cook a little even after it leaves the oven from its residual heat.

Coffee Cake

Manasa Kashi

Serves 6–8

125 g unsalted butter
125 g powdered white sugar
100 g all-purpose flour
25 g cocoa powder
¾ tsp baking powder
½ tsp salt
3 eggs
1 tsp vanilla essence
15 g instant coffee powder
¼ cup milk

Grease a 9-inch tin with butter and preheat the oven to 180 degrees Celsius. Sieve together flour, cocoa powder, baking powder, and salt. Ideally, do this thrice for maximum air incorporation. In a large bowl, beat butter (at room temperature) and sugar with a whisk until light and fluffy. In a separate bowl, beat vanilla essence and eggs until frothy. Add the flour mixture and the egg mixture to the butter and sugar mixture, and beat together. Slightly warm the milk and dissolve coffee in it. Pour into the batter and mix well.

Pour batter into the tin and bake for 18 to 25 minutes or until a toothpick comes out from the centre with 1 to 2 crumbs only.

Serve warm.

Notes:
—Most recipes will say to bake until the toothpick/skewer comes out clean, but if the toothpick is clean, it's a little too late. Cakes continue to cook even after they come out, right until they cool completely. So if the toothpick has 1 to 2 crumbs when you take it out, it will finish cooking by the time it cools. This is especially important in this recipe because it tends to run a little dry.

Rich Christmas Fruit Cake

Mandy Ridley

Serves family and friends over a number of days

225 g butter
100 g brown sugar
100 g caster sugar
4 eggs
½ cup sherry/whiskey/Cointreau
225 g all-purpose flour
50 g self-raising flour
A pinch of salt
3 level tsp mixed spice powder
1 ½ kg mixed dry fruits (raisins, sultanas, cherries, dates, figs, apricots) and nuts

Drizzle ½ cup alcohol on the dry fruits and nuts and keep in a sealed container at least overnight, but longer if you can.

Prepare the cake tin (ideally 20 cm in diameter and 8 cm deep) by lining it with 4 layers of brown baking paper. Preheat the oven to 150 degrees Celsius.

Sift both flours, salt, and spices. In a large bowl, cream the butter and and both sugars thoroughly. Beat in eggs one at a time. Add half the pre-soaked fruits and nuts and stir in lightly the sifted flour, and then the remainder of the soaked fruits and nuts. At this point all members of the household present should have a stir and make a wish.

Pour the batter into the prepared tin and place in the centre of the oven, covering the tin with a double thickness of brown paper; this is removed during the last ½ hour of baking. Bake at 150 degrees Celsius for about 4 hours.

Test the centre of the cake before removing from the oven: it should be firm to touch and when pierced with a shiny skewer, it should emerge quite clean. Your house should also smell delicious! Remove the cake from the tin, but not from the paper, and allow to cool. Leave the cake in the paper until cutting or icing.

Traditional Christmas cakes are iced with a layer of marzipan and then finished with royal icing before decorating.

Notes:
—From when I was a child this cake was made by my mother for Christmas. I often helped to cut the fruit into smaller pieces before it was soaked in sherry: the longer the soaking, the more fragrant the result. The recipe reflects the strong British influence on our cuisine. I now make this recipe for my own family for Christmas and special birthdays. Over the years there have been quite a number of these cakes baked and sent via Australia Post to our scattered family interstate. To get each family member to stir and make a wish is an important part of the process.

Black Forest Cookies

Ashok Vish

Makes 24 cookies

1 cup all-purpose flour
2 tbsp unsweetened cocoa powder
2 tbsp ground milk chocolate bar
1 tsp baking powder
½ tsp salt
225 g semi-sweet or bittersweet chocolate
½ unsalted butter
¼ cup granulated sugar
¼ cup dark brown sugar
2 eggs
350 g semi-sweet chocolate chunks
1½ cup dried cherries
2 cups brandy

Soak cherries in brandy for a day. Preheat the oven to 170 degrees Celsius. In a medium bowl, whisk flour, cocoa, ground chocolate bar, baking powder, and salt together and set aside.

Chop bittersweet chocolate and butter into small cubes and place in a large bowl. Set this over a pan of simmering water, but make sure the bottom of the bowl does not come into direct contact with the base of the pan. Stir until molten and smooth. Remove from heat and whisk in sugar, followed by eggs until smooth. Whisk in the dry ingredients just until combined, making sure you don't over mix it.

Fold in chocolate chunks and cherries. Press plastic wrap directly onto the surface of the dough and refrigerate until firm (for 30 to 45 minutes). Drop mounds of dough (equal to 2 tbsp), about 2 inches apart, onto a cookie sheet. Bake just until the edges are firm (but not darkening) for about 11 to 13 minutes.

Let it cool completely or serve while warm.

Notes:
—Instead of placing the bowl over a pan of simmering water, the process can also be done in a microwave in short increments.

Peanut Butter Blossom Cookies

Ashok Vish

Makes 24 cookies

1 ¾ cup all-purpose flour
1 tsp baking soda
½ tsp salt
100 g butter
½ cup smooth peanut butter
½ cup granulated sugar
½ cup light brown sugar
1 egg
1 tbsp milk
1 tsp vanilla essence
1 packet of Hershey's Kisses

Sift together flour, baking soda, and salt. Set aside. Using an electric mixer, cream together butter, peanut butter, granulated sugar, and light brown sugar. Add in the egg, milk, and vanilla essence and beat until well blended. Gradually add the flour mixture, stirring thoroughly. Refrigerate for about 1 hour.

Preheat the oven to 190 degrees Celsius. Spray or grease a cookie sheet with non-stick spray or butter. Roll the dough into 1-inch balls, then roll them in sugar, and place 2 inches apart on a cookie sheet. Bake until light brown and puffed (for 8 to 10 minutes).

Remove the sheet from the oven and lightly press a Hershey's Kisses into the centre of each cookie, allowing it to crack slightly.

Cool completely and serve.

BEVERAGES

Rum Punch ✦ Sangria ✦ Painkiller ✦ Cuba Libre ✦ Blood and Sand ✦
Jalapeño/Chilli-Infused Margarita ✦ Pomegranate Lime Vodka Cocktail ✦
Hot Toddy ✦ Spiced Rum

Rum Punch

Suresh Jayaram

Makes 16–20 glasses

750 ml Old Monk or Khodays XXX (or any dark rum)
500 ml orange juice
5 limes
2 l water
A small block of ice
A handful of mint leaves
2 cups black tea decoction
2-inch piece of ginger
1 apple
2 tsp salt
2 tbsp orange or lime rind

Grate ginger. Finely chop mint leaves and apple. Squeeze limes and keep the juice aside. Pour water into a punch bowl or any large container; stir in the orange and lime juice and add ice. Add in mint leaves, black tea decoction, ginger, and apple. Stir well and add in rum. Add 2 tsp of salt and garnish with orange or lime rinds.

Serve immediately, while cold.

Notes:
—This is a regular drink at 1Shanthiroad openings.

—Adding the rind will give it a slight bitterness.

—Tang or Rasna can be used instead of fruit juice.

—A variation can be made by using 1 large pineapple chopped, a 500 ml Tetra Pak of orange juice, 4 limes, and a bottle of soda and by following the same procedure.

—A Sangria-like variation can be achieved by replacing the rum with red or white wine.

Sangria

Ricardo Gallego

Serves 4

1 l red wine
½ l Old Monk (or any dark rum)
2 oranges
4 peaches
2 apples
1 sweet lime
5 tsp sugar
2 lemon rinds
2 cinnamon sticks
3 cloves
1 star anise

Wash peaches, apples, and sweet lime; peel their skin and cut into small cubes. Pour wine into a large bowl and add sugar, stirring until it is completely dissolved. Juice oranges into the bowl. Add in chopped fruits. Finally, add spices. Transfer the contents of the bowl into a jug (preferably a clay jug) and refrigerate overnight to let the fruits absorb the wine and sugar.

Just before serving, add in rum and a block of ice. Drink by cheering *Salud!*

Notes:
—You can cut a slice of a whole orange and use as decoration.

—If it isn't summer, the peach can be replaced with any fruit which you may have available that is not too soft.

—Rum can be substituted with any other hard drink—vodka, brandy, gin, or a mix of them.

—Here you have an authentic and traditional recipe for *sangria*—a wine-based cool drink for when the weather gets really hot. It has sparked joy to many openings at 1Shanthiroad. For openings or vernissages, make a minimum of 10 litres.

—Choose a red wine that is not too expensive. It doesn't matter if it has a high or low alcohol content. I recommend the home distilled red wine from the bakery in Johnson Market in Bangalore. You have to get acquainted with the owner to get him to sell it to you. Go a few days in advance to have *suleimani* tea and biscuits in the bakery, ask him about his family history, and only after a few meetings bring up the need to buy the wine.

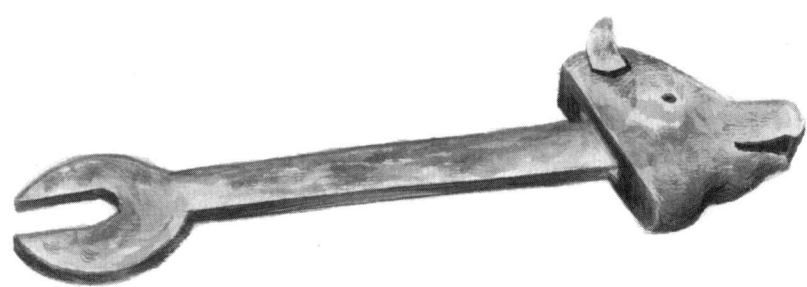

Painkiller

Ashok Vish

Serves 1

90 ml Old Monk (or any dark rum)
90 ml pineapple juice
60 ml orange juice
30 ml cream of coconut (or coconut milk)
A pinch of nutmeg powder
15–20 ice cubes

Fill a cocktail shaker or a big bowl with ice. Gather all the ingredients in a vessel or container. Pour the mixture into the cocktail shaker/bowl. Shake or stir well. Strain or pour into a glass with ice cubes.

Serve with a dash of nutmeg!

Notes:
—As a matter of personal choice and taste, you can alter the ratios of the rum and juices.

Cuba Libre

Ashok Vish

Serves 1

90–100 ml Old Monk (or any dark rum)
2 lime wedges
200 ml Coca-Cola
Ice cubes

Fill a glass with ice cubes. Squeeze and drop 2 wedges of lime into the glass, coating the ice cubes well with the juice—this makes a difference, ask the Cubans! Pour in rum and Coca-Cola.

Stir gently and serve!

Blood and Sand

Ashok Vish

Serves 1

30 ml whiskey
30 ml sweet vermouth
30 ml Heering cherry liqueur (or any other cherry liqueur)
30 ml orange juice
15 ml lime or lemon juice
Ice cubes

Prepare a chilled glass by placing it in the refrigerator or freezer for some time before making the drink. Pour whiskey, vermouth, cherry liqueur, orange juice, and lime/lemon juice in a shaker. Add ice cubes and shake well. Strain the drink into a chilled glass.

Serve cold.

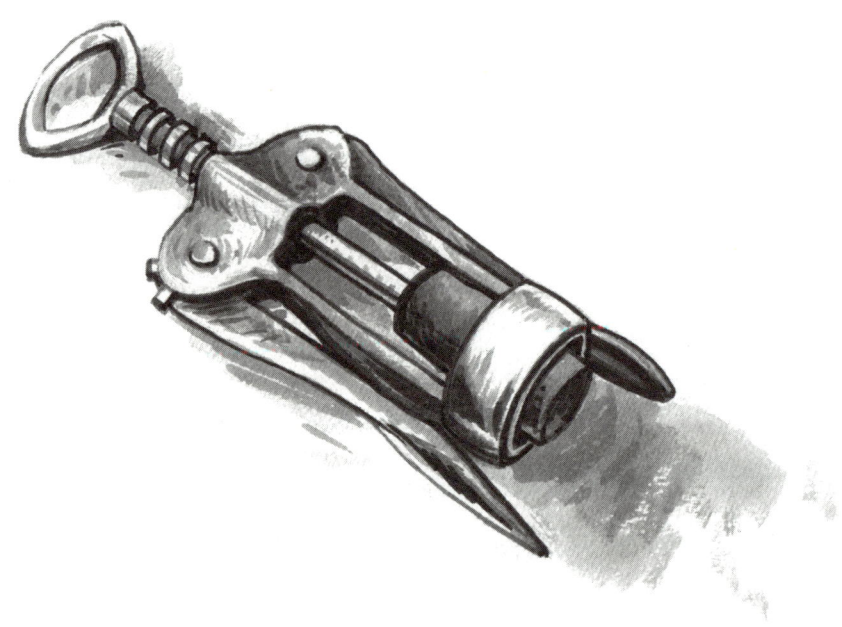

Jalapeño/Chilli-Infused Margarita

Ashok Vish

Serves 2

JALAPEÑO/CHILLI INFUSION:
1 bottle tequila
3 jalapeños (or 5 green chillies)

MARGARITA:
60 ml lemon juice
60 ml lime juice
15 ml triple sec
30 ml pineapple juice
Ice cubes

To infuse the tequila with jalapeño or chillies, slice 5 green chillies or 3 whole jalapeños and place at the bottom of a jar. Pour an entire bottle of tequila on top. Shake the jar for 30 seconds. Set it aside for 2 days (or up to a week). The longer it sits, the spicier it will get.

For the margarita, fill a shaker with ice cubes and pour in freshly squeezed lime juice and lemon juice. Then add pineapple juice, triple sec, and 80 to 100 ml of the jalapeño/chilli-infused tequila. Give it a good shake. Finally strain the cocktail into a glass with ice. If you like pulp, don't strain it and just pour everything in.

Serve cold.

Notes:
—To rim the glass with salt, scatter some salt onto a plate and set it aside. Now take an empty glass and smear the rim with a lime. Lastly roll or twist the rim in salt, by flipping the glass over, before you create your cocktail.

—Triple sec can be replaced with simple syrup based on availability.

—The lemon juice can be replaced with an extra 60 ml of lime juice.

Pomegranate Lime Vodka Cocktail

Shiva Syam

Serves 1

45 ml vodka
1 glass of fresh pomegranate juice
1 tsp simple syrup
2 tsp lime juice
5–10 pomegranate seeds
5–10 mint stalks
2 ice cubes
A slice of lime

In a cocktail shaker, add pomegranate juice, simple syrup, and lime juice, and shake well. Add ice and vodka; shake well again. Strain into a chilled cocktail glass. Garnish with a slice of lime, mint stalk, and pomegranate seeds.

Serve cold.

Hot Toddy

Shiva Syam

Serves 1

½ cup hot water
45 ml whiskey
2–3 tsp honey or sugar syrup
3 tsp lime juice
1 lime or lemon rind
1 cinnamon stick

In a cocktail shaker, add hot water, whiskey, honey, and lime juice and mix well. Pour into a whiskey glass, garnish with lemon rind and a cinnamon stick.

Serve hot.

Spiced Rum

Ashok Vish

Serves 3–4

2–3 tbsp brown sugar
2 limes
1 tsp cloves
4 cinnamon sticks
150 ml Old Monk (or any dark rum)
A pinch of salt
3 cups water
Orange juice to taste

Squeeze 2 limes and keep the juice aside. Bring 3 cups of water to a boil. To the boiling water, add brown sugar, lime juice, cloves, cinnamon, and a pinch of salt. Now simmer for about 7 minutes. Remove the pot from heat and add a dash of orange juice (to your taste) and the rum.

Strain and serve while it's still hot.

Notes:
—You can add cardamom pods as well and let the spices simmer for a few minutes longer for a spicier concoction.

PODIS AND FRESH MASALAS

South Karnataka Chutney Pudi ✦ Flax Seed Chutney Pudi ✦ Dry Peanut Chutney ✦ Kovakkai Poriyal Masala ✦ Bachelor Sambhar Powder ✦ Pepper Rasam Powder ✦ Upaddam Podi ✦ Kara Kozhambu Masala

South Karnataka Chutney Pudi

Anita Rao Kashi

Makes 500 g

1 cup *urad dal*
1 cup *chana dal*
2 cups dry red chillies
½ cup tamarind
2 cups grated desiccated coconut
½ cup curry leaves
½ cup coriander leaves
1 tsp mustard seeds
2 tsp jaggery powder
2 tsp salt
2 tsp groundnut oil
¼ tsp asafoetida

Clean the fibres of tamarind and tear it into little pieces.

In a wide wok or *kadhai*, dry roast *urad dal*, *chana dal*, and desiccated coconut, one by one, till lightly brown and aromatic, and keep aside to cool. Grease wok with a few drops of oil and roast red chillies broken in half until crisp and keep aside. Then roast curry leaves and coriander leaves separately till they lose moisture and turn dark, but take care not to burn. Lastly, add tamarind and quickly roast; it will stick so make sure to constantly stir.

Once all roasted ingredients have cooled, powder one by one and empty into a large bowl. Mix well, add salt, jaggery, and asafoetida and run it once again in the mixer-grinder. Heat remaining oil in a small *kadhai* and add mustard seeds. When the seeds splutter, remove from fire and pour over the powder. Mix well and let it stand till completely cool. Store in an airtight container.

Serve with hot rice and *ghee* or curd rice.

Notes:
—The jaggery powder is optional, depending on your preference.

—For medium-spicy *pudi*, opt for equal quantities of Salem (hot) and Byadagi (mildly hot, but rich in colour) chillies. Adjust spice levels by altering the proportion of the two varieties.

—Divide into batches and store the major portion in the freezer compartment of the refrigerator; it will not only last long but also remain fresh.

—Other ways of consuming include: mix with thick curd and finish with a *ghee*-mustard *tadka* to make chutney for *idli* and *dosa*. You can also make a quick snack by mixing together 1 tsp of *pudi*, a bowl of *puri* (puffed rice), 1 tbsp of grated coconut, 1 tbsp of chopped coriander leaves, 1 tsp of oil, and salt to taste.

Flax Seed Chutney Pudi

Anita Rao Kashi

Makes 500 g

1 cup flax seeds
¾ cup cumin seeds
2 tbsp *urad dal*
2 tbsp *chana dal*
2 tbsp grated desiccated coconut
1 cup dry red chillies
1 tbsp black peppercorns
1 cup curry leaves
1 cup tamarind
½ tsp jaggery powder
2 tsp salt
¼ tsp asafoetida
A few drops of oil

Clean the fibres of the tamarind and tear it into little pieces.

In a wide wok or *kadhai* dry roast flax seeds until they splutter and keep aside to cool. Then roast cumin seeds, *urad dal*, *chana dal*, and coconut one by one until lightly dark and fragrant; cool. Add 1 to 2 drops of oil and toast red chillies broken in half until crisp, followed by peppercorns; remove and keep aside to cool. Add curry leaves and roast until crisp and remove. Lastly, add tamarind and quickly roast by stirring constantly as it will stick a bit. Let everything cool completely. Powder each ingredient separately and empty into a large bowl. Add jaggery, salt, and asafoetida and mix well. Taste to adjust salt. Run in a mixer-grinder once more and store in an airtight container.

Serve mixed with hot rice and *ghee*, with *idli* and *dosa*, sprinkled on *upma*, and even as stuffing in layered *roti*.

Notes:
—Adjust heat levels by using a mix of Salem (hot) and Byadagi (mildly hot but provides rich red colour) chillies.

—Divide into batches and store a major portion in the freezer compartment of the refrigerator; it will not only last long but also remain fresh.

—Don't omit jaggery; it is required to counter the mild bitterness of flax seeds.

—A couple of spoons everyday is a delicious way to add flax seeds into the daily diet.

Dry Peanut Chutney

Rucha Vibhute

Makes 400g of chutney powder

300 g peanuts
8–10 cloves of garlic
Salt to taste
3 tbsp of red chilli powder
½ tsp sugar
1 tsp cumin seeds
2 tsp peanut oil

Dry roast peanuts in a pan over a low flame, cool, and remove the skin.

In a pan, heat oil and add cumin seeds, roasted peanuts, red chilli powder, and garlic and fry until fragrant. Once the mixture is cool, transfer the ingredients to the mixer-grinder, add salt and sugar, and grind to a coarse powder. Do not run it in the mixer-grinder for long, as it will become a paste. Store in an airtight container. It can last upto 15 days.

Serve as an accompaniment to *roti*, rice, bread, or *khakra*. Preferably serve mixed with *ghee*, oil, or curd.

Notes:
—You can adjust the quantity of chilli powder according to your taste.

—Peanut oil can be replaced with any vegetable or sunflower oil.

—The same recipe can be made without garlic.

—For a variation, peanut can be replaced with coconut.

—Another variation can be made with green chillies, peanuts, cumin seeds, and salt. After this is ground into a coarse paste, roast it in a pan till the moisture is gone and it turns crispy.

Kovakkai Poriyal Masala

(Ivy Gourd Poriyal Masala)

Ramalingam VK

Makes 100 g

12 dry red chillies
4 tsp coriander seeds
1 tsp black peppercorns
4 tbsp peanuts
1 tsp cumin seeds

Dry roast each ingredient separately and let them all cool. Then, mix the ingredients and grind them in a mixer-grinder (or mortar and pestle) to produce a coarse powder.

This *masala* powder is used to make *kovakkai* roast *poriyal*—a dry preparation of chopped ivy gourds, tempered with curry leaves and mustard seeds, and slow cooked with a pinch of salt and turmeric powder. Add 3 tsp of this powder to 250 g of ivy gourd while it cooks, mix well, and let it roast.

This powder can also be used while making other *poriyals* with vegetables like brinjal, raw banana, potatoes, *arbi*, okra, snake beans, and broad beans.

Bachelor Sambhar Powder

Ramalingam VK

Makes 100 g

15 dry red chillies
2 tsp coriander seeds
1 tsp cumin seeds
½ tsp black peppercorns
2 tsp *chana dal*
¼ tsp fenugreek seeds
1 tsp turmeric powder
¼ tsp asafoetida

Dry roast each ingredient (except turmeric powder and asafoetida) separately and let them all cool. Then, mix the ingredients with turmeric powder and asafoetida and grind in a mixer-grinder (or mortar and pestle) to produce a fine powder.

This *masala* powder is used to make *sambhar*—a thin gravy of vegetables and *toor dal* cooked in tamarind water, tempered with curry leaves, mustard seeds, and a pinch of asafoetida. Add 3 tsp of this powder into the simmering gravy when making *sambhar* for 4 people.

Pepper Rasam Powder

Ramalingam VK

Makes 150 g

4 tbsp black peppercorns
2 tbsp cumin seeds
2 tbsp coriander seeds
1 tbsp *toor dal*
1 tbsp turmeric powder

Dry roast each ingredient (except turmeric powder) separately and let them all cool. Then, mix the ingredients with turmeric powder and grind in a mixer-grinder (or mortar and pestle) to produce a fine powder.

This *masala* powder is used to make pepper *rasam*—a hot, tangy, thin, and spiced soup, with its tangy flavour coming either from tamarind extract, lime juice, or tomatoes. It is tempered with *ghee*, curry leaves, cumin seeds, and a pinch of asafoetida. Add 3 tsp of this powder into 750 ml water, when making the dish for 4 people.

Upaddam Podi

Sarasija Subramanian

Makes 200 g

8 tbsp raw rice
1 tbsp fenugreek seeds
3 dry red chillies
2 tbsp sesame seeds

Dry roast each ingredient separately and let them all cool. Then, mix the ingredients and grind in a mixer-grinder (or mortar and pestle) to produce a coarse powder.

This rice-based *masala* powder is used as a substitute for *sambhar* and *rasam* powders (which are usually lentil-based) and as a thickening agent for tamarind-based curries. It is specifically used in *uppadam*—a traditional Palakkad dish of sautéed okra cooked in a watery tamarind extract, tempered with curry leaves, mustard seeds, fenugreek seeds, and a pinch of asafoetida. Add 2 tbsp of this powder to 750 ml water when making this dish for 4 people.

Kara Kozhambu Masala

(Spicy Kozhambu Masala)

Ramalingam VK

Makes 100 g

12 dry red chillies
4 tsp coriander seeds
1 tsp cumin seeds
1 tsp black peppercorn
2 tsp *chana dal*

Dry roast each ingredient separately and let them all cool. Then, mix the ingredients and grind them in a mixer-grinder (or mortar and pestle) to produce a coarse *masala* powder.

This *masala* powder is used to make *kara kozhambu*—a curry with vegetables (usually brinjal, okra, red pumpkin, or shallots) simmered in a thick tamarind extract and tempered with curry leaves, mustard seeds, and garlic. Add 3 tsp of this powder into the simmering gravy, when making the dish for 4 people.

Glossary

(Left to right: English, Hindi, Kannada)

GRAINS AND FLOURS

Broken rice	—	*Akki nuchchu*
Coarse rice flour / Rice semolina	*Dardara chawal ka atta / Chawal ka rava*	*Akki tari*
Finger millet flour	*Nachni atta*	*Ragi hittu*
Fried gram flour	*Sattu*	*Hurgadale hittu*
Gram flour	*Besan*	*Kadale hittu*
Pearl millet flour	*Baajra ka atta*	*Sajje hittu*
Pounded wheat	*Kuta hua geehun*	*Godhi nuchchu*
Red rice flour	*Lal chawal ka atta*	*Kempakki hittu*
Refined wheat flour / All-purpose flour	*Maida*	*Maida hittu*
Rice	*Chawal*	*Akki*
Rice flour	*Chawal ka atta*	*Akki hittu*
Semolina	*Rava*	*Reve*
Tapioca pearls	*Sabudana*	*Seeme akki*
Wheat flour	*Gehun ka atta*	*Godhi hittu*

PULSES, LEGUMES, AND LENTILS

Black chickpeas	*Kala chana*	*Kadale kaalu*
Black gram / Split black lentils	*Urad dal*	*Uddina bele*
Black-eyed beans / Cowpeas	*Lobia*	*Halsande / Alasande bele*
Chickpeas	*Kabuli chana*	*Kabul kadale*
Fresh pigeon peas	*Tuver na dana / Toor*	*Thogarikai*
Fried gram	*Bhuna chana dal*	*Hurgadale*
Horse gram	*Kulthi dal*	*Huruli*
Hyacinth beans	*Surti papdi / Sem ki phali*	*Avarekai*
Mung beans	*Moong dal*	*Hesaru bele*
Pigeon peas	*Toor dal / Arhar dal*	*Thogari bele*
Split chickpeas	*Chana dal*	*Kadale bele*
Split red lentils	*Masoor dal*	*Masoor bele*

VEGETABLES

Beetroot	*Chukandar*	—
Brinjal	*Baingan*	*Badanekai*
Broad beans / Flat beans	*Baakala phali*	*Chapparadavare*
Cabbage	*Patta gobi*	*Yele kosu*
Capsicum	*Shimla mirch*	*Donamenasinakai*
Carrot	*Gaajar*	—
Cauliflower	*Phool gobi*	*Hookosu*
Celery	*Ajmod*	—
Cluster beans	*Gavar phali*	*Gorikai*
Cubanelle pepper	*Bajji mirch*	*Bajji menasinakai*
Drumsticks	*Sehjan*	*Nuggekai*
French beans	—	*Hurulikai*
Green peas	*Matar*	*Batani*
Indian gooseberry	*Amla*	*Nellikai*
Ivy gourd	*Kundru / Tindodi*	*Thondekai*
Kohlrabi	*Knol khol*	*Gedde kosu*
Lima beans / Double beans	—	*Double beans*
Mangalore cucumber	—	*Dosekai / Mangaluru southekai*
Mushroom	*Kukurmutta*	*Anabe*
Okra	*Bhindi*	*Bendekai*
Onion	*Pyaaz*	*Eerulli*
Potato	*Aloo*	*Alugedde*
Radish	*Mooli*	*Mullangi / Moolangi*
Raw banana	*Kaccha kela*	*Balekai*
Ridge gourd	*Tori*	*Heerekai*
Shallots	*Chhota pyaaz*	*Sambhar eerulli*
Snake beans	—	*Halasandekai / Alasandekai*
Snake gourd	*Chichinda*	*Padavalakai*
Spring onions	*Hara pyaaz*	*Eerulli kaavu*
Sweet corn	*Bhutta*	*Musukina jola*
Sweet potato	*Shakarkand*	*Genasu*
Taro root	*Arbi*	*Shaave gedde / Kesavina gedde*
Tomato	*Tamatar*	—
White pumpkin / Ash gourd	*Petha*	*Buda kumbalakai*
Yam	*Suran / Jimikand*	*Suvarna gedde*

GREENS

Amaranth leaves	*Chaulai*	*Dantina soppu*
Dill leaves	*Dill / Sua bhaaji*	*Sabbaki / Sapsige soppu*
Fenugreek leaves	*Methi bhaaji*	*Menthye soppu*
Mountain spinach	—	*Chakotha*
Roselle leaves	*Ambadi bhaaji*	*Gongura soppu*
Spinach	*Palak*	*Palak soppu*

FRESH HERBS AND SEASONING

Basil leaves	*Tulsi*	*Tulasi*
Coriander leaves	*Dhaniya patta*	*Kothambari soppu*
Curry leaves	*Kadi patta*	*Karibevu*
Garlic	*Lehsun*	*Bellulli*
Ginger	*Adrak*	*Shunti*
Green chilli	*Hari mirch*	*Hasiru menasinakai*
Lemon	*Bada nimbu*	*Gajanimbe*
Lime	*Nimbu*	*Nimbe hannu*
Mint leaves	*Pudina patta*	*Pudina soppu*
Raw tamarind	*Kacchi imli*	*Hunasekai*

FRUITS

Apple	*Seb*	*Sebu*
Banana	*Kela*	*Baale hannu*
Coconut	*Nariyal*	*Tenginakai*
Desiccated coconut	*Copra*	*Kobbari*
Green grapes	*Angoor*	*Hasiru drakshi*
Jackfruit	*Katahal*	*Halasina hannu/kai*
Mango	*Aam*	*Mavina hannu*
Orange	*Santara*	*Kitthale hannu*
Peach	*Aadu*	—
Pineapple	*Ananas*	*Ananas*
Pomegranate	*Anaar*	*Daalimbe hannu*
Raw mango	*Kaccha aam*	*Maavinakai*
Sweet lime	*Mosambi*	*Mosambi*
Tender coconut	—	*Yalaneeru*

SPICES AND CONDIMENTS

Allspice	*Kabab cheeni*	*Gandamenasu*
Asafoetida	*Hing*	*Ingu*
Bay leaves	*Tej patta*	*Palav yele*
Black cardamom	*Badi elaichi*	*Kari ellaki*
Black peppercorn	*Kali mirch*	*Kari menasu*
Black salt	*Kala namak*	*Kari uppu*
Byadagi chillis	—	*Byadagi menasinakai*
Capers	*Kabra*	*Mullu kattari*
Caraway seeds	*Shahi jeera*	*Shahi jeera*
Carom seeds	*Ajwain*	*Om kalu*
Cinnamon	*Dal cheeni*	*Chakke*
Clove	*Laung*	*Lavanga*
Coriander seeds	*Sabut dhaniya*	*Kothambari beeja*
Cumin seeds	*Jeera*	*Jeerige*
Dried fengreek leaves	*Kasuri methi*	—
Dry red chilli	*Lal mirch*	*Kempu menasinakai*
Fennel seeds	*Saunf*	*Sompu*
Fenugreek seeds	*Sabut methi*	*Menthya*
Garcina indica / Garcinia cambogia	*Kokum / Goraka*	*Kachumpuli / Kudampuli*
Green cardamom	*Elaichi*	*Elakki*
Honey	*Shahad*	*Jenu thuppa*
Jaggery	*Gud*	*Bella*
Kapok bud	*Shalmali / Semul*	*Marathi moggu*
Mace	*Javitri*	*Jakai patre*
Mustard seeds	*Sarson*	*Sasive*
Nigella seeds (onions seeds)	*Kalaunji*	*Eerulli beeja*
Nutmeg	*Jaiphal*	*Jakai*
Pandanus extract	*Kewra paani*	—
Rock salt	*Sendha namak*	*Kalluppu*
Rose water	*Gulab jal*	—
Saffron	*Kesar*	*Kesari*
Salt	*Namak*	*Uppu*
Salty-curd chillies	—	*Mor-milagai / Majjige menasinakai / Balaka*
Sesame seeds	*Til*	*Yellu*
Sichuan / Szechuan pepper	*Timur*	—

Star anise	*Chakra phool*	*Ananas hoova*
Sugar (castor)	*Cheeni*	*Beesida sakkare*
Tamarind	*Imli*	*Hunasehannu*
Turmeric powder	*Haldi*	*Arishina*

SEEDS, DRY FRUITS, AND NUTS

Almonds	*Badam*	*Badami*
Apricot	*Khubani*	*Sakkare badami*
Cashew nuts	*Kaju*	*Godambi*
Dates	*Khajoor*	*Karjura*
Figs	*Anjeer*	*Anjura*
Flax seeds	*Alsi*	*Agase beeja*
Peanuts	*Moongphali*	*Kadalekai*
Pine nuts	*Chilgoza*	—
Poppy seeds	*Khus khus / Posta dana*	*Gasagase*
Pumpkin seeds	*Kaddu ke beej*	*Kumbalakai beeja*
Raisins	*Kishmish*	*Vana drakshi*
Sunflower seeds	*Suryamukhi ke beej*	*Suryakanthi beeja*
Walnuts	*Akhrot*	*Akhrot*

OILS

Coconut oil	*Nariyal ka tel*	*Kobbari yenne*
Gingelly / Sesame oil	*Til ka tel*	*Yellenne*
Groundnut oil	*Moongphali ka tel*	*Kadalekai yenne*
Sunflower oil	*Suryamukhi ka tel*	*Suryakanti yenne*

DAIRY

Butter	*Makkhan*	*Benne*
Buttermilk	*Chaas*	*Majjige*
Claified butter	*Ghee*	*Thuppa*
Cream	*Malai*	*Kene*
Milk	*Doodh*	*Haalu*
Yoghurt / Curd	*Dahi*	*Mosaru*

POULTRY, FISH AND MEATS

Beef	*Gomaans*	*Gomaamsa*
Carp	*Rohu*	—
Country chicken	*Murga*	*Naati koli*
Egg	*Anda*	*Motte*
Mackerel	*Bangda*	*Bangda*
Mutton	*Bakre ka maans*	*Kuri maamsa*
Mutton chops	—	*Chaaps*
Pork	*Shookar maans*	*Handi maamsa*
Seer fish	*Surmai*	*Anjal*
Small prawns	*Jhinga machli*	*Sigadi*
Tuna	*Choora*	*Gedare*

EQUIPMENT

Iron skillet	*Tawa*	*Kavali / Henchu*
Wok	*Kadhai*	*Baandle*
Tempering spoon	—	*Vaggarnay soutu*

Contributors

Aaiushi Beniwal is an artist based in Baroda. She was an artist-in-residence at 1Shanthiroad Studio/Gallery in 2016 as part of the Next-Step Residency, supported by the Sher-Gil Sundaram Arts Foundation.

Aishwaryan K is an artist based in Bangalore. He was the programme coordinator at 1Shanthiroad from 2011 to 2012.

Amshu Chukki is an artist and filmmaker based in Bangalore. He is part of the extended family of friends of 1Shanthiroad.

Anita Rao Kashi is an independent journalist and a travel and food writer based in Bangalore. She is part of the extended family of friends of 1Shanthiroad and is the consulting editor of this book.

Ankit Ravani is an artist based in Bangalore. He is part of the extended family of friends of 1Shanthiroad.

Anna Mary Magdalene is an LGBTQIA rights supporter based in Kochi. She is part of the extended family of friends of 1Shanthiroad.

Archana Hande is an artist based in Bangalore. She is a regular collaborator in 1Shanthiroad's projects.

Arshad Hakim is an artist and filmmaker based in Bangalore. He was an artist-in-residence at 1Shanthiroad in 2015.

Arshi Irshad Ahmadzai is an artist based in Delhi and Kabul. She was an artist-in-residence at 1Shanthiroad in 2019, with support from the Inlaks Shivdasani Foundation.

Arundhati Ghosh is the executive director of India Foundation for the Arts. She is part of the extended family of friends of 1Shanthiroad.

Arunesh Maiyar is a hospitality consultant based in Bangalore. He is part of the extended family of friends of 1Shanthiroad.

Ashok Vish is a filmmaker and film curator based in Bangalore. He was the programme coordinator at 1Shanthiroad from 2016 to 2019.

Ayisha Abraham is an artist and filmmaker based in Bangalore. She is part of the extended family of friends of 1Shanthiroad.

Babu Eshwar Prasad is an artist and filmmaker based in Delhi and Bangalore. He is part of the extended family of friends of 1Shanthiroad.

Barblina Meierhans is a composer and sound artist based in Zurich and Berlin. She was an artist-in-residence at 1Shanthiroad in 2013, with support from Pro Helvetia.

Basavachar S is an artist and printmaker based in Bangalore. He is part of the extended family of friends of 1Shanthiroad.

Benjamin Buchanan is an artist based in Te Whanganui-a-Tara. They were an artist-in-residence at 1Shanthiroad in 2014, with support from the Asia New Zealand Foundation.

Bharathesh GD is an artist based in Bangalore. He is a regular collaborator in 1Shanthiroad's projects.

Bhavani GS is an artist based in Bangalore. She participated in the Sethusamudram Project and is a regular collaborator in 1Shanthiroad's projects.

Birte Hendricks is a contemporary dancer based in Berlin. She was an artist-in-residence at 1Shanthiroad in 2018.

Biju Cherayath is an artist and graphic designer based in Bangalore. She is a regular collaborator in 1Shanthiroad's projects.

Bilal Javeed is a business professional based in Bangalore. He is a founding trustee of Reliable Copy and is part of the extended family of friends of 1Shanthiroad.

Devi Raju has been the chief cook at 1Shanthiroad since 2005 and is an integral member of the 1Shanthiroad family.

Dimple B Shah is a multidisciplinary artist based in Bangalore. She was one of the participants in the Sethusamudram Project.

George Demir is an artist based in Cologne. He was an artist-in-residence at 1Shanthiroad in 2017 as part of the BangaloREsidency, supported by the Goethe-Institut.

Heena Pari is an artist based in Bangalore. She is part of the extended family of friends of 1Shanthiroad.

Dr. Hemalatha Bhuvanendra is a doctor and 1Shanthiroad's next door neighbour. She is Suresh Jayaram's elder sister.

Jahangir Asgar Jani is an artist based in Mumbai. He was an artist-in-residence at 1Shanthiroad in 2011.

Janet Burchill & Jennifer McCamley are artists based in Melbourne. They were artists-in-residence at 1Shanthiroad in 2009, with support from Asialink's Arts Residency Programme.

Janet Meaney is a performance artist based in Canberra. She was an artist-in-residence at 1Shanthiroad in 2012, with support from Asialink's Arts Residency Programme.

Jayasimha Chandrashekar is a printmaker based in Bangalore and the founder of Atelier Prati, a printmaking studio. He is part of the extended family of friends of 1Shanthiroad.

Julia D Kjelgaard is an artist based in Atlanta. She was an artist-in-residence at 1Shanthiroad in 2006, with support from a Fulbright Fellowship.

Kadamboor Neeraj is an artist and writer based in Baroda. He is part of the extended family of friends of 1Shanthiroad.

Dr. Lakshmi Devi was a doctor, homemaker, and chef by passion. She was Suresh Jayaram's mother and a founding trustee of VAC Trust that administers 1Shanthiroad.

Lina Vincent is an art historian and curator based in Goa. She is part of the extended family of friends of 1Shanthiroad.

Manasa Kashi is a student at an alternative school in Bangalore. She was one of the research assistants for this book and is part of the extended family of friends of 1Shanthiroad.

Mandy Ridley is an artist based in Brisbane. She was an artist-in-residence at 1Shanthiroad in 2006, with support from Asialink's Arts Residency Programme.

Mariraj Rajasekaran is an artist based in Hyderabad. He was an artist-in-residence at 1Shanthiroad in 2018 as part of the Next-Step Residency, supported by the Sher-Gil Sundaram Arts Foundation.

Maureen Gonsalves is the cultural coordinator at Goethe-Institut / Max Mueller Bhavan, Bangalore. She is part of the extended family of friends of 1Shanthiroad.

Miya Shivaram is a theatre artist based in Kochi. She is a member of a transgender drama company and is part of the extended family of friends of 1Shanthiroad.

Mohanavathi V has been the resident caretaker of 1Shanthiroad since its founding in 2003 and is an integral member of the 1Shanthiroad family.

Murari Jha is an artist based in Delhi. He was an artist-in-residence at 1Shanthiroad in 2015.

Muskaan Singh is an artist based in Delhi. She was an artist-in-residence at 1Shanthiroad in 2018 as part of the Next-Step Residency, supported by the Sher-Gil Sundaram Arts Foundation.

NS Harsha is an artist based in Mysore. He has been on the advisory board of 1Shanthiroad since its founding in 2003.

Nihaal Faizal is an artist based in Bangalore. He is the publisher of Reliable Copy and was an artist-in-residence at 1Shanthiroad in 2015.

Omana Eappen is an art connoisseur based in Bangalore. She is part of the extended family of friends of 1Shanthiroad.

Pradeep Kambathalli is an artist based in Bangalore. He was one of the participants in the Sethusamudram Project.

Pushpamala N is an artist and curator based in Bangalore. In 2010, she initiated the Re-Look Series of talks at 1Shanthiroad.

Raghu Tenkayala is a cultural administrator based in Bangalore. He was the programme coordinator at 1Shanthiroad in 2005.

Ragini Bhow is an artist from Bangalore currently based in New Mexico. She was an artist-in-residence at 1Shanthiroad in 2014.

Ramalingam VK is a hotelier by profession and chef by passion. He is part of the extended family of friends of 1Shanthiroad.

Renu Appachu is a social worker and the founding director of Jagruthi Foundation. She is a founding trustee of VAC Trust.

Ricardo Gallego is a business professional based in Pune. He is part of the extended family of friends of 1Shanthiroad.

Rohini Sen is an artist based in Bangalore. She is part of the extended family of friends of 1Shanthiroad.

Rucha Vibhute is a researcher and archivist based in Bangalore. She is part of the extended family of friends of 1Shanthiroad.

Sandeep TK is an artist and photographer based in Bangalore. He has been the programme coordinator at 1Shanthiroad since 2014.

Sapna Chandu is an Australian-Indian interdisciplinary artist based in Melbourne. She was an artist-in-residence at 1Shanthiroad in 2013.

Sarasija Subramanian is an artist based in Bangalore. She is the editor at Reliable Copy and was an artist-in-residence at 1Shanthiroad in 2018.

Shanthi Kasi is an artist and photographer based in Mumbai. She was an artist-in-residence at 1Shanthiroad in 2017.

Sheela Gowda is an artist based in Bangalore. She is part of the extended family of friends of 1Shanthiroad.

Shiva Syam is a photographer and ex-bartender based in Bangalore. He is part of the extended family of friends of 1Shanthiroad.

Shivaji Panikkar is an art historian based in Baroda. He is part of the extended family of friends of 1Shanthiroad.

Shubham Kumar is an artist based in Baroda. He was an artist-in-residence at 1Shanthiroad in 2019 as part of the Next-Step Residency, supported by the Sher-Gil Sundaram Arts Foundation.

Shyamli Singbal is an artist based in Goa. She was an artist-in-residence at 1Shanthiroad in 2017 as part of the Next-Step Residency, supported by the Sher-Gil Sundaram Arts Foundation.

Sitikanta Samantsinghar is an artist based in Delhi. He was an artist-in-residence at 1Shanthiroad in 2018 as part of the Next-Step Residency, supported by the Sher-Gil Sundaram Arts Foundation.

Smitha Cariappa is a performance artist based in Bangalore. She is part of the extended family of friends of 1Shanthiroad.

Sohail Abdullah is an artist based in Karachi. He was an artist-in-residence at 1Shanthiroad in 2008, as part of the KHOJ @ 1Shanthiroad South Asian Residency.

Sunil Sigdel is an artist based in Pokhara. He was an artist-in-residence at 1Shanthiroad in 2010, as part of the KHOJ @ 1Shanthiroad South Asian Residency.

Thisath Thoradeniya is an artist based in Colombo. He was a collaborator in the Sethusamudram Project, an international exchange programme between 1Shanthiroad and Theertha International Artists Collective.

Thomas & Renée Rapedius are artists based in Berlin. They were artists-in-residence at 1Shanthiroad in 2010, with support from the Goethe-Institut.

Tim Wolfgarten is an academic researcher based in Cologne. He is part of the extended family of friends of 1Shanthiroad.

Tsohil Bhatia is an artist based in Pittsburgh. They were an artist-in-residence at 1Shanthiroad in 2016 as part of the Next-Step Residency, supported by the Sher-Gil Sundaram Arts Foundation.

Umesh Kumar is an artist based in Bangalore. He is a regular collaborator in 1Shanthiroad's projects.

Uwe Jonas is an artist and the coordinator of Lichtenberg Studios in Berlin, a partner organisation to 1Shanthiroad. He was an artist-in-residence at 1Shanthiroad in 2015.

Yugashri Anandappa is an artist based in Bangalore. She is a regular collaborator in 1Shanthiroad's projects.

Suresh Jayaram is an artist, art historian, arts administrator, and curator, whose practice involves urban mapping, archiving, and arts education. He is the founding director of 1Shanthiroad Studio/Gallery, a non-profit arts organisation based in Bangalore, India. He previously taught art history at the Karnataka Chitrakala Parishath in Bangalore, where he was also the Dean between 2005 and 2007.

1Shanthiroad Studio/Gallery is Bangalore's oldest running non-profit residency and arts space. Founded by Suresh Jayaram in 2003, it is administered under the Visual Arts Collective (VAC) Trust and has functioned for the last nineteen years as a venue for exhibitions, residencies, screenings, lectures, presentations, and performances, as well as an open house to its many visitors. As a space of collective gathering, 1Shanthiroad, through its location in—and emphasis on—Bangalore, exhibits a unique relationship to the city.

Reliable Copy #4
The 1Shanthiroad Cookbook
Suresh Jayaram • 2020

Reliable Copy is a publishing house and curatorial practice for works, projects, and writing by and with artists. It is represented by Nihaal Faizal and Sarasija Subramanian and operates under Reliable Copy Trust, in association with Press Works.

Reliable Copy Trust & Press Works,
14/2, Andree Road,
Shanthi Nagar,
Bangalore – 560027,
Karnataka, India

www.reliablecopy.org